P9-CEI-972

Praise for Alison Leslie Gold's

Memories of Anne Frank
Reflections of a Childhood Friend

★ "Gold explores the world of Anne Frank to bring home the painful truths that Frank has come to symbolize.... the poignancy of Gold's book rests in its sensitive evocation of Goslar's youthful reactions to the war and its destruction of her family and community. Readers feel Goslar's desolation and shock upon discovering the Franks' disappearance.... Gold uses carefully chosen details and specific incidents to communicate the horrors of the Holocaust. While acknowledging frequent cruelty, she emphasizes the heroism and altruism of prisoners.... Readers drawn to Anne Frank's diary will be grateful for the fuller picture rendered here."

—*Publishers Weekly,* STARRED REVIEW

"*[Memories of Anne Frank]* reads like a haunting version of what Anne's life could have been.... This survivor story intensifies the ordinariness of Anne's diary and the arbitrariness of her death."　　　　　—*Booklist*

"This straightforward account will satisfy the diary's international readership on two counts: first, it extends the information we have about Frank; and second, it deepens our knowledge of her situation through Pick-Goslar's own experiences in Nazi-occupied Amsterdam and of surviving both transit and concentration camps.... Pick-Goslar's story... is involving in its own right."　　—*Bulletin of the Center for Children's Books*

POLARIS

A new direction in nonfiction.

We Shall Not Be Moved
The Women's Factory Strike of 1909
by JOAN DASH

An American Hero
The True Story of Charles A. Lindbergh
by BARRY DENENBERG

Winning Ways
A Photohistory of American Women in Sports
by SUE MACY

Malcolm X
By Any Means Necessary
by WALTER DEAN MYERS

Memories of Anne Frank

Reflections of a Childhood Friend

Alison Leslie Gold

SCHOLASTIC INC. NEW YORK · TORONTO · LONDON · AUCKLAND · SYDNEY

Photo credits:
Title page: UPI Corbis-Bettmann (Anne Frank)
Insert: Photo 1 used by permission of Jan Wiegel. Photos 2, 3, 4, 5, 6, 7, 8, and
10 used by permission of Hannah Pick-Goslar. Photo 11 used by permission of
Gay Block.

No part of this publication may be reproduced in whole or in part, or stored in
a retrieval system, or transmitted in any form or by any means, electronic, mechanical,
photocopying, recording, or otherwise, without written permission
of the publisher. For information regarding permission, write to Scholastic Inc.,
555 Broadway, New York, NY 10012.

ISBN 0-590-90723-9

Copyright © 1997 by Alison Leslie Gold. All rights reserved. Published by Scholastic Inc.
POLARIS, SCHOLASTIC, and associated logos are trademarks and/or registered trademarks of
Scholastic Inc.

12 11 10 9 8 7 6 5   1   8 9/9 0 1 2 3/0

Printed in the U.S.A.   23

This book is dedicated to the children and grandchildren of Hannah Pick-Goslar and to Hannah's son-in-law Shmuel Meir, Deputy Mayor of Jerusalem, who died tragically on December 3, 1996. It is also dedicated to Miep Gies, who protected Anne Frank.

Author's Note

In 1993 I met Hannah Elizabeth Pick-Goslar in Jerusalem, Israel. We spent many hours together while she told me everything she could remember about her childhood friendship with a girl she grew up with in Amsterdam, Holland, named Anneliese Marie. Hannah and Anneliese lived next door to each other from age four to age thirteen until World War II came to Holland. One day with no warning Anneliese and her family abandoned everything they owned, asked their lodger to feed their cat, and disappeared.

Hannah Goslar gave me permission to write about her memories of her friendship with Anneliese and of her own struggle during the war. World War II was a bewildering time of cruelty and persecution. It was long ago, so it was often very painful and difficult for Hannah to remember these times. Where words and happenings were not remembered exactly, they're described as accurately as Hannah could recall them.

We did the interviews in English, which Hannah had learned as a schoolgirl over fifty years ago. Because I want the book to sound like Hannah, sometimes the style is a little cryptic.

There are things that make the story of this friendship quite startling. One is that Hannah's friend Anneliese died of disease and starvation as a prisoner in a concentration camp only a few weeks before the end of the war, when she was not quite sixteen years old. Though she died, Anneliese's diary survived the war. It is also startling that Hannah's childhood friend Anneliese, whose nickname was Anne, was Anne Frank. Anne's diary remains as one of the most important documents of the entire war.

When Anne Frank's diary was published in Holland in 1947 many of the names were changed to protect the privacy of real people. This is how Hannah Elizabeth Goslar became "Hanneli" or "Lies" in *Anne Frank: The Diary of a Young Girl.*

After Nazi Germany was defeated at the end of World War II, Holland was liberated. Germany became a free country again, too. In 1947 Hannah emigrated to Israel. In Israel she became a nurse and married Dr. Walter Pinchas Pick. They had three children, and at last count, ten grandchildren.

Otto Frank, Anne's father, who was the only

member of the Frank family to survive the war, sent Hannah Goslar one of the first copies of Anne's diary after it was published. Can we imagine how Hannah felt when she read her name many times in Anne's diary? Can we imagine how Hannah felt when she read the entry Anne wrote on November 27, 1943, which recounts in poignant detail a dream Anne had about Hannah while she was in hiding? The dream is so prophetic, it's almost eerie and it expresses Anne's concern and tenderness toward Hannah, her oldest childhood friend.

Anne and Hannah were ordinary girls. They were just like any young people, giggling in class, whispering secrets. But because of the war Anne wrote her extraordinary diary while she and her family were hiding from the Germans. Miep Gies, Mr. Frank's employee, who risked her life to care for them while they were hiding, rescued the now famous diary after Anne and her family were arrested and imprisoned. During the course of the war, Hannah and her family were also imprisoned.

Like Anne, Hannah was brave and endured brutality and tragedy. These tragic times brought about extraordinary attributes in both young girls whose childhood friendship and growing up was abruptly interrupted. Anne died just before her sixteenth birthday and Hannah was already sixteen when the Germans surrendered. It was by sheer luck that Hannah survived at all.

There is no way to explain how young girls like Hannah Goslar and Anne Frank found the strength to endure horrific suffering and utter hopelessness, or to convey what gave Anne Frank the gift to interpret these terrible times so movingly.

After Anne had been in hiding for two years she wrote on July 15, 1944, that although she saw so much destruction and felt so much human misery around her, she fervently believed that misery and cruelty would one day finish and world peace would replace world war.

Anne was right. World War II did end and peace did return to the world. Tragically though, Anne and most of her family were destroyed as were most of Hannah's family. Though Anne's diary remains, the cruelty these young girls endured remains to haunt us all.

Note by Hannah Pick-Goslar

This story about my youthful friend Anne Frank and myself is an important story for children as well as for adults. But to go through this painful remembrance again and again, and tell about this awful time, even with the support of the writer Alison Leslie Gold, I had to have a reason.

Anne wrote in her diary on November 27, 1943, about me: She asked why should I (Anne Frank) be chosen to live and she (Hannah Goslar) probably to die? Ironically the opposite came true. Now I am a happy grandmother in Israel, and it was Anne who died. Because of this irony I feel obliged to tell as much as I can about Anne Frank. Anne wanted to be famous and to live on after her death. By telling what I remember, perhaps I can add a little to her fame, though Anne never would have dreamed how famous she is now.

After such a long time I've tried to remember things as exactly as possible, but Anne and I were friends beginning over sixty years ago and it is hard to remember everything exactly. Sometimes I can remember exact words, sometimes I can't. What is written in this book is as close to what I can remember as possible. Of course I couldn't know that the whole world would be interested in every small detail of Anne's youth. If I had known that Anne would be so famous, I'd have tried to remember better. At the time of our childhoods she really was a girl like other girls her age, only her development was much quicker and her writing very mature.

I once asked our late headmistress, Mrs. Kuperus, if she had seen something special in Anne. It was her opinion that a child who you close off from the whole world, from her friends, from nature, from flowers, from animals, from everything, who lives under such unreal circumstances with people older than herself, like Anne did while in hiding, will develop much quicker than in regular circumstances. Perhaps she was right.

Anne's diary reveals the deepest part of my friend which, because of her tragic death, no one would ever have known if the diary hadn't miraculously been preserved. But Anne's diary has no ending; it stops right in the middle one morning when

Anne and the others in hiding were arrested by the Nazis. Perhaps this book will add to the knowledge of Anne Frank, will fill in what really happened—as horrible as it was—to my friend after the diary ends.

Mrs. Hannah Pick-Goslar
Jerusalem, Israel

CHAPTER ONE

On Tuesday morning, July 7, 1942, after a day of heavy rain, the sun came out in South Amsterdam, Holland. Hannah Goslar was dressed for summer in a light cotton dress. The school year was finished, the graduation ceremony had been the previous Friday. The days were now long and the sky was probably filled with big puffy Dutch clouds.

Hannah's mother had sewn the yellow six-pointed star—which all Jewish people had been ordered to wear—to the front of Hannah's dress above her heart. The Star of David usually made Hannah feel proud to be Jewish, but because Jews were now being arrested and persecuted by the Germans who had conquered Holland, it made her conspicuous, like a target at a shooting range.

At age thirteen Hannah Goslar was fun-loving but also quite religious. She went to Hebrew school two times a week and to synagogue. She was gangly, tall, had creamy skin, and brushed her mahogony-brown hair so fast that electric sparks crackled.

Hannah's best features were her hair and her soft, brown eyes.

This morning she was going to call for her friend Anne Frank. Anne was outspoken, even impudent; she loved having fun. She was more interested in socializing and boyfriends than Hebrew lessons. Lately the differences between Hannah and Anne had become more pronounced. With the war raging and both of them being thirteen, life was not as simple as it used to be when they were little girls sitting side by side at school.

Hannah had kissed her father before she left the house. Because of a new law that Jews were forbidden from working in most professions, Mr. Goslar was no longer allowed to work as a professional economist. This meant it was difficult for him to support his family.

They'd had to move to a building on Zuider Amstellaan, next door to where her grandparents lived. It was around the corner from where they used to live next to the Frank family. Her father barely could care for them by doing odd bits of translating work, giving consultations to other refugees, and recently by making ice cream with an Italian man named Mr. Giroudi, who sold the ice cream in a cart.

Her father was fair-haired with hazel eyes. He

had long since finished his morning prayers and was drinking his morning coffee. "All taste has gone out of life," he told her. "This coffee is tasteless. The Nazis steal everything tasty and send it back to Germany."

When Mr. Goslar went back to his newspaper Hannah could see that he was fretting again. Since Germany had conquered Holland her parents worried night and day. Now that the Nazis had begun to arrest Jewish people, they anguished even more.

Hannah kissed her baby sister, Gabi, and went to find her mother.

Mrs. Goslar, who was pretty (and knew Latin, Greek, and even English), was on the little balcony above the garden helping Irma, a refugee girl, shake the threadbare carpet over the railing. Irma lived in a little room in their apartment and was supposed to help Mrs. Goslar in return for room and board. Since Irma was a little retarded Mrs. Goslar had to help her do even simple things.

Often these days Mrs. Goslar was irritable. Deep down she was dreaming that one day they would all go back to Germany where they had once lived. She missed thick Persian carpets, strong German coffee, and speaking in the German language.

Mrs. Goslar was going to have another baby

quite soon. When Hannah hugged her she could barely get her arms all the way around. Hannah always told her mother everything. When she would tell her some little thing that Anne had said, Mrs. Goslar usually commented, "God knows everything but Anne knows everything better." And then they'd laugh because Anne was such a know-it-all and thought it odd that Hannah confided so freely in her mother.

As Hannah was about to leave, Mrs. Goslar asked her to get Mrs. Frank's scale because she was going to make strawberry jam from one of the little packets containing pectin that Mr. Frank's company manufactured for jam making and which the Franks gave to them. She needed a scale to weigh the ingredients. Hannah promised she would.

"Take care, Hanneli!" her mother cautioned. "The Germans are picking up Jews on the street and sending them to God knows where."

CHAPTER TWO

Hannah walked briskly along the sidewalk lined with old trees. Dozens of Amsterdammers were on their way to work, peddling on their black bicycles. On the street were German soldiers with faces as hard as cement. The soldiers' gloves were tucked into their belts, their rifles hung over their shoulders. They looked intently at the faces of passing people. But feeling the warm sunlight and smelling the fresh air Hannah forgot the danger and felt like a beautiful bird that had fluffed out its feathers.

She met their friend Jacque and together they walked to the building where Anne lived. For nine years, before they'd moved, the Goslar family had lived next door to the Frank family. Anne and Hanneli had been able to call to each other from window to window. Hannah hoped that Anne and she might iron out what was prickly between them, that distance that was hard to put her finger on.

Hannah whistled the usual two notes that she and Anne had whistled for years. She hoped that after she'd run home with the scale for her mother, she could hear all about the sleepover that she'd missed in order to help her mother with Gabi. Then maybe a game of Monopoly.

What was wrong between them? Lately, Anne had gotten closer to Jacque. Though Jacque was reserved, she was more sophisticated than the rest of them. Also, Anne was madly in love with several boys at once. At the same time, Hannah had a boyfriend named Alfred Bloch who was three years older. Alfred was the rabbi's nephew and lived with the rabbi.

Hannah couldn't say she was madly in love with Alfred, but he was definitely her boyfriend. She could feel her cheeks get warm when she was with him and he had confessed that he felt the same way about her. Hannah also had a new girlfriend. Her name was Ilse Wagner and, though all the girls were friendly, Hannah and Ilse went to synagogue together.

At Anne's house, no one came to the door so Jacque and Hannah waited and rang the bell once more.

Recently their Ping-Pong club had met and had a sleepover at Anne's. Their club was named The Little Dipper Minus Two. The reason they'd added "minus two" to the name was because the dipper had seven stars and there were only five of them in the club. At the sleepover, when they were getting undressed, Anne had showed Hannah and the other girls that she was wearing one of her sister Margot's old bras and that some cotton was stuffed inside to round it out. The other members of the club burst out giggling.

Of course Jacque didn't need such tricks; she was much more developed than any of the others. At these sleepovers the talk often turned to private goings-on between grown-up men and women. If it wasn't the stomach where babies come from, where was it, they wondered? Talking about such things always made them collapse into fits of giggling.

They impatiently rang the bell again. Anne never took this long to answer the door.

Still there was no answer.

They were just about to leave when Mr. Goldschmidt, the bachelor who rented a room from Anne's parents, opened the door and asked what they wanted. Hannah explained that her mother had sent her to borrow a scale and that she and Jacque wanted to see Anne.

The sun was shining on their faces and arms. Were the Franks out? They couldn't have gone swimming because Jews weren't allowed in public pools anymore.

"Don't you know that they've gone?" he asked the girls. "They left yesterday in the rain. I think they went to Switzerland. Mr. Frank has business associates there, his mother lives there. That's where they must have gone."

Hannah and Jacque looked at each other with disbelief. Mr. Goldschmidt pulled the door entirely open so they could go into the apartment and look if they didn't believe him. They walked in and saw that everything was as it had always been, all the furniture, all the Franks' belongings were there. The dining room table was filled with dishes.

Mr. Goldschmidt handed Hannah the scale. She and Jacque walked right through the sitting room straight into Anne's room. Feelings of panic were welling up in Hannah. Wouldn't Anne have told them if she were going away? Wouldn't Anne have taken her scrapbooks with her if she were going away?

When she looked she saw that, yes, the scrapbook that was filled with pictures of movie stars and children of kings and queens was gone from Anne's shelf. The red-checkered diary that Anne had just gotten for her thirteenth birthday was also gone. A few clothes were gone, the bed was stripped down, but most everything else, including her new shoes and swimming medals, were left behind.

Moortje—Anne's cat—walked soundlessly into the room. Moortje let out a long, lonely meow. They knew that Anne would never leave Moortje. Mr. Goldschmidt told them the Franks had left a pound of meat for the cat and he would feed her, then he would find a neighbor to take her in. They walked out of the room and to the front door.

On the threshold of the apartment Moortje stopped and sat up on her haunches. She was faithfully waiting for Anne to appear from around the corner.

Hannah felt a wave of hatred toward the Nazis, even though violence and hate were against her religion and upbringing. If the Nazis hadn't conquered Holland, didn't persecute Jewish people, the Franks wouldn't have fled the country that they liked so much. It was impossible to hold back the flood of tears and the sensation of panic. Both she and Jacque were stunned that their friend and her entire family had simply vanished.

CHAPTER THREE

Hannah hugged the metal scale in her arms. Just before she reached her building she saw Alfred hurrying toward her. He told her, "I was at your house. I came to say good-bye."

He looked quite nervous. He explained that he had gotten an order from the Germans to report for forced labor, that he would be leaving for Germany immediately. He wanted to say good-bye.

Where in Germany?

He told her that he didn't know, probably he would be sent to a work camp.

Would his uncle be going with him?

No. His uncle, the rabbi, hadn't received a summons. Only he had. He'd have to report alone.

Alfred was panic-stricken. He was only sixteen. If only he could get away, to Spain, or across the mountains to Switzerland. If only he could find a hiding place, find someone kind to hide him from the Nazis. Though he tried to appear brave, fear oozed out of his being, and Hanneli wished there was something she could do for him.

Tearfully, Hanneli said good-bye. Alfred promised to write and they agreed to meet after the war. Yes, she assured him, she'd be his girlfriend when he returned.

Quickly he was gone.

At lunch Hannah stared down at her sandwich.

Anne's lucky," Mrs. Goslar exclaimed. "If only we had some way to leave. We'd vanish, too! Who knows if we'll be picked up and shipped to God knows where for forced labor like poor Alfred? The rabbi must be out of his mind with worry."

Outside it began to rain. As usual Mr. Goslar went out to visit friendless old people at the Joodse Invalide Hospital. The disappearance of the Frank family had put Mrs. Goslar's nerves even more on edge. After all, she and her husband were close friends of Mr. and Mrs. Frank. They celebrated holidays together and drank coffee together.

Mrs. Goslar was pale and had dark circles under her eyes. She lost patience because Gabi was a finicky eater. Irma was hopeless with Gabi. Mrs. Goslar asked Hannah to feed the baby for her so that she could sit down, drink a cup of coffee, and smoke a cigarette.

Hannah did as she was asked, though Gabi liked to clench her little sharp teeth against the spoon. When Hannah filled the spoon, she began the game she always played with Gabi to get her to eat.

"One spoonful for me."

Gabi would open her mouth and swallow the food.

"One for Mama . . ."

Gabi would open again.

Afraid that luck would run out, she would speed up, "One for Papa."

Gabi would open so the spoon could slide in.

"One more for me!"

But Gabi sometimes clamped her mouth closed because the rule of the game was that Hannah must not mention the same person twice. "Then one for Alfred!" she exclaimed and felt a big lump in her throat. Where were they sending him? Would he be safe? Would he be treated decently?

Outside the rain poured down. Hannah read Gabi one story after another. In the afternoon she realized that so much had happened she was unprepared for Hebrew school. How could she be a good scholar when she had to take care of Gabi so much of the time? She felt like a bird had nested in her chest.

After lunch she sat in the kitchen with her mother and helped weigh the fat strawberries for jam. On the wall was a painted ceramic tile that Alfred had made and given to her. It showed the Wailing Wall in Jerusalem. He'd given her another tile, also painted, but with a scene of a waterfall. Hannah was proud of Alfred's ceramics; Anne had admired them, too.

Her mother cooked the fruit down for jam, and added sugar and pectin from the packet to thicken the fruit. June was the month the farmers sold strawberries. Every year Hannah and Anne had smeared slices of bread with tasty strawberry jam. It seemed like any second Anne would come bursting in, sit down, and make a joke about Hanneli having two left hands.

To make Hanneli laugh Anne might do her trick of taking her shoulder out of its socket. Whenever Anne did this people would gasp, then have a good laugh. For sure the girls would taste big spoonfuls of the sweet and bubbling fruit stew that boiled on the stove, then Anne would probably begin chattering outrageously about her many boy-friends, and Mrs. Goslar would shake her head and raise her eyebrows.

CHAPTER FOUR

At bedtime Hannah's parents came into her room and said good night. She wondered if they knew something about Anne's family they weren't telling her. Would her mother and father lie to her? Her mother reminded her to put the night guard on her teeth before she went to sleep. Hannah had to wear these braces every night. The idea was that they would straighten her teeth while she slept.

Anne had just disappeared and already Hannah had a list of things she wanted to tell her. Like: Alfred had been ordered into a forced labor brigade and was being shipped to Germany. How impatient her mother had been with her a few days before. Hannah knew that Anne would understand since Anne's mother also got impatient these days. She wanted to tell Anne about the royal cards she'd traded with someone, one Princess Elizabeth of York for a Prince Gustav.

Hannah took the family photo album that stood on the shelf and opened it. At the beginning of the book were photos of Mr. and Mrs. Goslar. They were smiling, young, newly married. There were photos of their years in Berlin, where they had lived until the Nazis had taken control of Germany. Like the Franks, who had come from Frankfurt, Germany, when Anne was four years old, the Goslars had come to Holland from Berlin, Germany, when Hannah was also four years old.

There were photos of Amsterdam, photos of Hannah and Anne alone and with friends at various ages. There was a photo of Hannah and her parents and grandparents.

There were photos of Gabi. Gabi was born just as the German army had attacked then-occupied Holland in 1940. Despite the war, Gabi's arrival had made everyone happy.

There was a photo of the thatched cottage on the North Sea in which the Goslars rented rooms during the summer. Anne came to stay with the Goslars during the holiday. The cottage was a little white guest house with a black thatched straw roof. Because the guest house served only vegetarian food, Hannah and Anne had nicknamed it the Tomato House.

One time while at the seaside Mr. and Mrs. Goslar took the girls to an amusement park. They were about eight years old. Hannah and Anne had stood in front of crazy mirrors. The mirror made them look enormously fat like circus ladies and they had laughed. After the mirrors they'd watched how ceramics were shaped then put in an oven and baked. They were each given a little piggy bank made of ceramic.

That very evening the girls were left alone in the cottage because Mr. and Mrs. Goslar went for a walk. There came a terrible thunderstorm that made great cracking explosions. The lightning ricocheted across the sky. Anne had cried. She was afraid because her own parents were so far away.

There were other photos.

But now Anne was gone. How frightened Anne must be. Hannah was frightened, too, and she was in her own bed. Alfred must be packing his rucksack, saying good-bye to his uncle. He must be afraid, too. They were all scared when they woke up, scared when they went to bed, scared by every noise. But now everything had gotten even worse.

The room was dark. Though it was illegal, Hannah peaked out from behind the blackout shade that covered the window. The dark street glistened with puddles. The searchlight beams pointed up at the sky, looking for enemy airplanes.

High up, the engines of hundreds of airplanes made droning noises. At night, planes flew over

Holland to bomb German cities and villages. Her father had told her that the British were bombing Cologne, the German city on the Rhine River. Hannah thought how somewhere Anne, Anne's older sister Margot, and Edith and Otto Frank, were making an escape across dangerous mountains to Switzerland where they would be safe.

She wondered how they would sneak across borders that were controlled during wartime by the Germans. Would they be stopped? What would happen if they were caught? Could they be shot? Could they be put in a concentration camp where they had heard harsh conditions awaited them?

Searchlights crisscrossed the sky making ghostly stripes against the clouds. The muffled *ack ack* sound of antiaircraft guns in the distance could be heard. Hannah thought that wherever the Franks were tonight, Anne must be as afraid as she had been during that summer thunderstorm when they were little.

Hannah closed the blackout shade and got under the cover. The room was very dark indeed.

CHAPTER FIVE

Sanne Ledermann was the president of The Little Dipper Minus Two Club, Jacque, the secretary. Ilse Wagner, Hannah, and Anne were the founding members of the club.

Sanne had grown up with them. She was quiet, smart, always fun. Ilse and Jacque had recently moved into their circle. Jacque's mother was French. She worked in a posh shop and the other girls thought she was very chic. Ilse was reserved and pious.

The purpose of the club was to play Ping-Pong and gossip. But whenever the girls gathered after Anne's disappearance, they were gloomy. They wondered if Anne was in Switzerland yet. They imagined the Franks on a train. They wondered if Anne had dyed her hair, done things to not look Jewish. Of course they also worried that the Franks might have been caught.

They would sit moodily missing their friend. Hannah remembered that before Anne left, the

club had met in Ilse's dining room. The Ping-Pong
set was adjusted to fit the table. Because it was such
a hot day, the Ping-Pongers had been very lazy.
Finally they had stopped trying to play and sunk
into chairs.

One of the girls had suggested that the Ping-
Pongers adjourn their meeting for ice cream. With
their arms around each other's shoulders, the club
members had trooped around the corner to the
Oasis. The Oasis was a Jewish-owned ice-cream
parlor and tearoom where Jews were still allowed to
go. Jews had already been banned from most
restaurants, tea shops, hotels, public parks, public
swimming pools, and most shops.

They ordered ice cream for twelve cents. They
also kept their eyes open for cute-looking boys
from the neighborhood who might wander by.

Later at the sleepover at the Franks', Mrs.
Frank had served donuts that she had baked. She
always offered food and treats to Anne's friends.
She served the donuts she made every year on New
Year's Eve. Hannah knew the donuts well because
every year since they'd known each other the tradi-
tion had been that one of them would sleep at the
house of the other on the last day of the year.

Each year Hannah and Anne alternated. At
midnight the parents would wake them up. Then

they would listen to the church bells ringing in the new year. When they were at Anne's house, Mrs. Frank would serve these tasty donuts. Remembering that sleepover, Hannah thought that Anne must not have known they were leaving. She couldn't have acted so normally if she had.

The friends agreed that when the war was over, and Anne came back, the club would meet again. Then Anne would tell them everything about her dangerous escape to Switzerland.

CHAPTER SIX

All summer things got worse. Four hundred Jews—from the old Jewish Quarter of Amsterdam—were arrested. Their poor neighborhood was encircled by soldiers, then these people were loaded into trucks, driven to trains, and had disappeared.

At night, Hannah would double-check that the door was locked. She lived in fear of a knock at the door in the middle of the night. During the day everyone could hear the fierce engines of Hitler's Luftwaffe Air Force. To retaliate against the English, the Luftwaffe had begun flying massive daytime raids on England.

Each week Mr. Goslar read in the *Joodse Weekblad* the new anti-Jewish laws. To protect Hannah, he didn't discuss what he read. Late at night, though, he and his wife whispered about the new, unjust laws. He forgot that the same decrees were plastered on posters in the street and, of course, Hannah saw them.

Jewish bank accounts were frozen; individual

people, both Jews and non-Jews who didn't agree with the Nazis, were constantly being arrested for no reason at all. They heard that people who were arrested were sometimes beaten, kicked, and insulted.

During the day, while Hannah and Ilse walked to synagogue together, flocks of pigeons would fly into the air when the metallic drone of airplanes was heard. The bombers were flying above the thick clouds that always filled the Amsterdam sky.

❦

One hot night, Hannah, Mr. Goslar, and Gabi sat together at the dinner table with her grandmother, grandfather, and Irma. Mrs. Goslar served noodles cooked with margarine since butter had gotten too hard to find. Mrs. Goslar told Hannah that she and her husband could no longer hide the danger from her. Her mother told her about the newest law: Jews would only be allowed into shops for two hours each day, from three to five. By then all the fresh food would be gone.

Then food rationing started. This meant that coupons were needed to buy very limited quantities of food. It became hard for Mrs. Goslar to find the makings of a proper meal for her family. Sometimes, in fact, she was too tired to shop at all. Her pregnancy was approaching its end and she was very weary, so she often asked Hannah to go shopping for her.

One time, Hannah was returning from the vegetable shop. She walked on familiar cobblestones set in a herringbone pattern when she saw an older couple she knew by sight being stopped by soldiers. She knew that right before the war these people had used their entire life savings to arrange papers and passage for their grown children and grandchildren to go to America. Now they were alone and penniless.

"Your identity card!" the soldier barked.

People crossed the street or hurried off. What would the soldier do when he saw the "J" for Jewish stamped inside their identity cards?

"Come with me!" the soldier shouted after he'd examined their cards.

Hannah felt her stomach clench as the couple was shoved toward an open truck. The soldier hit the old man who wore glasses directly in the face when he didn't move fast enough. Hannah's feet were like cement blocks. Her heart pounded.

Hannah's face was white as flour; her knees were buckling. Hannah wished that her family and all the Jews would run away while there was still time.

A few weeks later the Germans started surprise roundups of Jews right in South Amsterdam. These roundups were called *Razias*. Not only were they rounding people up in the old, poor quarter of Amsterdam, but now they had begun roundups in the Goslars' own neighborhood, too.

Her father told them about a family he knew from the synagogue who had been arrested. He explained that these people were separated from each other and deported for use as slave labor.

What if I got separated from Mama and Papa? Hannah thought in terror.

Her mother told her that the Jews who ran the bread shop had tried to run away but had been caught and the people upstairs were looking for a place to hide, a "safe" address. A "safe" address was a place protected by Dutch people who were willing to risk their lives to help Jews. Mrs. Goslar wished that the Franks had taken them along with them.

The following week Mr. Goslar came home in an excited mood.

"Look," he said as he opened a document with official stamps. "I've had some good luck. I've gotten a South American passports for us!"

Hannah was astonished.

"Paraguay is the name of the country in South

America. Maybe we'll be able to get out of Europe now."

When Hannah looked blank, he laughed. He reached into the bookcase and brought over a book of maps. Turning to a map, he pointed to a land-locked country right in the center of South America. He showed her that its main city was called Asunción. "In case you get asked, you should know the capital of Paraguay at least," he advised.

Then he produced another official-looking document and explained that because of his high position back in Germany they'd been put at the top of the Palestine lists to go to the Holy Land. There were over forty lists and they were on the second list.

Mrs. Goslar became exuberant. "I need a cup of coffee."

Going toward the kitchen to make coffee with a bit of real coffee she'd been saving for a special occasion, Hannah heard her father—for the first time in a long time—whistling melodies from his beloved Beethoven concerto.

CHAPTER SEVEN

Summer passed. In September school began again. Going to school was not the same with Anne gone. Hannah walked with other friends, but everyone's nerves were jumpy because of the *Razias*. It was strange to walk to school without Anne. The other girls were nice, but she felt lonely. No one was spicy like Anne, no one teased her like Anne did, and there was no one she could tease back.

Hannah often thought about the last time she and Anne had walked together along these same streets to school. It had been a Friday, the end of last June, a very important day. They had left for school a little early because it was the day their examination results would be announced. It was also the very last day of school before the summer vacation began.

Hannah had wondered aloud whether or not her reports would be passing. Anne had assured her that they'd be no worse than her own. Anne had tossed the thick dark hair that she was so proud of.

26

She hadn't been worried at all because her parents put very little stock in grades. Other students joined them and they all walked along together.

Truckloads of soldiers rattled past the group of children who were wearing yellow stars. The batch of bright yellow stars could have been a swatch taken out of the Milky Way. At the rattle of wheels, startled seagulls flew up into the sky, making little urgent cries. Pedestrians hurried to clear the streets. These Dutch people had to swallow the hate they felt for the soldiers that bullied them.

Was there trouble coming?

The truck crossed a bridge and bounced along the narrow cobbled street. Immediately, at signs of trouble, Jewish children hurried toward the Jewish Lyceum on Stadstimmertuinen Street.

In school both Hannah and Anne got promoted but—because they both had done so poorly in mathematics—they were told they would have to take the math examination for a second time after the vacation.

But that was long ago, last June.

This day, to cheer themselves up along the way to school, the friends joked that probably Anne was somewhere up in the Swiss Alps sipping hot chocolate at that very moment and was probably in love with a handsome boy. And he, of course, would be madly in love with her, too. They laughed.

Sometimes a man wearing the wolf trap emblem that supporters of Hitler wore would scrutinize the yellow stars. The way things were going, it was getting more dangerous to be apart from one's parents all day. Perhaps it was better that Anne had gone. At least Anne was no longer trapped in Amsterdam at the mercy of the Nazis.

❧

Autumn days became short. The weather turned wet and unpleasant. Alfred had not been heard from since he'd reported for forced labor. Wherever he had gone, he obviously was not allowed to write letters to her.

Hannah took the mathematics examination that she and Anne were to have taken again. She was very worried, but somehow passed.

At school each morning Hannah looked around her classroom. Not only Anne's chair but two or three more chairs were empty each week. When the teacher called out the name belonging to the vacant seat, he looked up from his book and asked if anyone knew what had happened to the missing student. No one knew. All they knew was that—like Anne Frank—another school friend had vanished, and after a week or two the teacher would stop including that name in roll call.

Who will be next? Will it be me? Will it be my family? Hannah wondered. All the children wondered. Sometimes in the afternoon she saw Jacque. She felt closer to Jacque. Why was I so jealous of Jacque? she wondered.

They'd all been together at Anne's birthday party on Sunday, June 14. Hannah remembered the party very well: It had been on the Sunday after Anne's actual birthdate, which was on June 12. Their school friends had trooped into Anne's apartment. It had been a hot day. Hannah had worn her prettiest dress.

When the sitting room had been filled with children, Anne had looked happily around the room full of friends eating, drinking, chattering, and became exhilarated. Mr. and Mrs. Frank filled china plates with slices of Mrs. Frank's special strawberry tart, and poured glasses of milk.

Margot looked very beautiful that day. Anne and Hannah thought of Margot as perfect. They envied her grown-up eyeglasses that made her even prettier and intelligent-looking. Margot was bright, obedient, quiet, and serious. She was good at mathematics and everything else. Not like them. Margot was the kind of perfect daughter every mother wanted. Not like them.

After the refreshments the shades were pulled down and a movie was shown, using the wall as a screen. The film was called *The Lighthouse Keeper*, starring the German shepherd dog named Rin Tin Tin. Rin Tin Tin leaped out of nowhere and rescued the imperiled lighthouse keeper and his little child.

No longer allowed into public movie theaters, this was the only way Jews could see a movie. They'd cheered for Rin Tin Tin to take the villain by the throat and drag him down onto his knees— just what they'd all like to do to the Nazis.

Anne would have loved to have had a dog like Rin Tin Tin. Hannah didn't want a dog; she was afraid of them. She preferred Rin Tin Tin in a movie rather than bounding across the room and sniffing her shoes. The other non-dog-lover— Moortje the cat—had swished her tail and haughtily left the room.

After the film Hannah had to go and help her mother with Gabi, as Irma had a headache. She went to find Anne to say good-bye, but Anne was nowhere in sight. Finally she had found Anne with Jacque. Their heads had been together, and they had been whispering and giggling. When Hannah had come close the whispering stopped.

"Good night," Hannah had said and wished Anne happy birthday once again.

Anne told Hannah she'd see her the next morning to walk to school and Hannah had left.

Looking back to the hot day of Anne's birthday, Hannah thought, Yes, I was jealous of Jacque! I didn't want to share Anne with Jacque. If I'd known what was going to happen, I wouldn't have minded. I wouldn't have been so immature. She felt regretful, but it was too late. Anne was gone.

CHAPTER EIGHT

❧

Early one evening while Hannah was doing the washing up in the kitchen, her father came in. He had heard that another tramload of sixteen-year-old children had been shipped to forced labor. These children were all the age of Alfred Bloch and Margot Frank. Mr. Goslar told them that the parents were not allowed to wave good-bye to their children, not even from the doorways of their homes. The Nazis had forbidden it.

Mrs. Goslar sighed gloomily. Hannah washed the dishes slowly, carefully. Then she heard her father lamenting, "Don't they know that human life is sacred?"

On her way to bed she saw her mother sitting at the kitchen table smoking one cigarette after another. Cigarettes were very hard to get these days, and though Mrs. Goslar loved coffee more than anything else, the ration for coffee was too small to even count.

Mr. Goslar stood wearing his skullcap. He

didn't smoke at all and didn't like seeing his wife smoke while she was pregnant. He was deep in prayer.

By October, very few children remained in Hannah's class. Hannah and the other children changed their seats to be closer to each other. One Thursday, her teacher informed them that there was good news. Someone with an illegal radio had told him that the Germans had been defeated in North Africa.

And—though it was against the law to speak of a German defeat—it was as though the sun was pouring in and all the children felt suddenly tall in their seats. Does Anne know the good news wherever she is? Hannah wondered.

On the way home, still exalted, Hannah looked down and saw several ration cards for coffee. She picked them up and gave them to her mother the second she opened the door. The joy her mother had when she drank the precious cups of coffee was worth every bit of danger involved in using ration cards that weren't their own.

But then a huge *Razia* took place in the old Jewish Quarter. This time not hundreds but thousands were arrested and taken away. Mrs. Goslar cried, "I know we'll be next! If only Otto and Edith Frank had taken us with them."

Mrs. Goslar was becoming more and more depressed.

When Mr. Goslar came home his wife sank into the sofa and sobbed. After he'd comforted her and told her to lie down, Hannah stood beside him while he made a hole in the wall with a knife. She helped while he put important papers and his wife's jewelry into the hole. Then he closed up the hole and covered it with a wall hanging. Next he tore up papers that might be dangerous. These he stuffed into the toilet. After each handful Hannah pulled the chain and flushed the shreds of dangerous paper down the drain.

❦

On a chilly day in winter, Hannah's teacher was sick. Mr. Presser, the history teacher, took his place. Mr. Presser began discussing the Renaissance. He explained that the Renaissance marked the transition from the medieval world to the modern world.

Then he went on to talk about the Italian writer named Dante. He explained that Dante first met Beatrice in 1274. Beatrice was the love, the guiding-star, the inspiration of Dante's life. Mr.

Presser stopped abruptly. He couldn't go on. He put his face down into his hands and sobbed.

Stunned by the sight of their teacher's shoulders shaking, all the children put their pens down and sat very quietly.

Mr. Presser took a handkerchief from his pocket. He blotted his eyes, got up, and walked out of the room. The children sat in their chairs. After a while Mr. Presser returned and told them that his wife had been taken away the night before. Then he dismissed the class.

The next day Mr. Presser didn't return. He, too, had disappeared and a new teacher was found.

As more Jews disappeared from their homes, and their possessions were seized, Dutch Nazis moved into the empty apartments. One day Ilse Wagner and her family were among those arrested and taken away. Hannah became even more frightened and missed Ilse terribly.

CHAPTER NINE

An explosion was heard. In the kitchen, to earn a few gulden, Mr. and Mrs. Goslar were huddled over the kitchen table translating some legal documents into German for another refugee. Was Amsterdam being bombed? No one could tell.

If Amsterdam was being bombed, their family could not go to a public air-raid shelter because Jews were forbidden from entering them. All anyone could do was pray. Though there were no more explosions that night, a new fear—the fear of bombs—had been kindled. Someone with a hidden radio learned that a British plane carrying explosives had crashed into the Carlton Hotel in the center of Amsterdam.

Sometimes coming home from school Dutch people who noticed the yellow stars on the students' coats would give them smiles of support. Hannah sometimes passed close to 37 Merwedeplein, where

Anne had lived, and where she once had lived at number 31. They had once leaned out the windows, whistled, and called back and forth to each other, winter, summer, autumn, spring. The windows had been thrown open and they had shouted freely.

Now the windows of the brown brick apartment buildings with sloping orange roofs looked forbidding, unfriendly. Jewish children never shouted at each other these days, lest they call attention to themselves. People whispered now, always looking scared and intimidated.

When Hannah got home from school her mother was moaning in bed. Her father was hovering over her. Hannah sat on the edge of her mother's bed, clenching her hands together. Mrs. Goslar told her, "I think the time for the new baby has come."

Seeing Hannah's distress, Mrs. Goslar reminded her that childbirth could be difficult, but it was worth it. She kissed Hannah. "Don't be afraid, Hanneli, after all, childbirth brought me you! What could be bad about it?"

The sweat was wetting and matting her mother's hair and the collar of her nightgown. Because there was no coffee left, Hannah made ersatz tea for her mother and father. Her hands were trembling when she carried in the cups. Mr. Goslar was grateful and drank it scalding hot. Mrs. Goslar was in too much pain to drink but told Hannah to stay close.

Then her mother apologized for being short-tempered sometimes and told her she hoped Hannah knew it was just because she'd been feeling so poorly. "Yes, Mama," Hannah reassured her. Her mother's pillow was soaking wet from sweat.

Shortly after, the nurse came and shut her mother's door behind her. To make the time pass Hannah counted and recounted her collection of rings from cigars. She turned the pages of her stamp collection. She spread out her Hebrew schoolbooks on the floor but instead of studying, she straightened out her collection of cards of the king of England's children—Princess Elizabeth of York and Princess Margaret Rose.

The Dutch royal children were in exile in England with Queen Wilhelmina. Beatrix was sweet-looking at four years old. There was a new princess—Irene—younger than Gabi. Because she had been born in exile, no one knew what the princess looked like.

Prince Baudouin and Prince Albert of Belgium were both very cute to look at. The most handsome was little Carl Gustav of Sweden, but he was much too young to look at twice.

From outside, as always, came the sound of shrill whistles and heavy hobnailed boots. Soldiers with skull and bone insignias on their caps marched along the streets with their rifles held against their chests.

The Frank family would be so happy that her mother was having the baby! She reminded herself that Anne was not going to be there to see the new child. But now there would be eight mouths to feed including Grandmother and Grandfather and Irma.

When her father came in to say good night she could see from his face that her mother wasn't doing well. He put on his prayer shawl and prayed all night. Hannah prayed, too.

In the morning her father told her she'd better go to synagogue because it was the Sabbath. The doctor had come. Her father kissed her. He was very worried about his wife since the labor was taking so long. Hannah worried all the way to and from synagogue.

When she returned and opened the door her father took both her hands in his. "Mama died in childbirth. So did our new baby."

Hannah's knees gave way. She started to collapse but her father caught her and clasped her as tightly as he could in his long, bony arms. Gabi started crying for milk.

With each passing hour, they cried more, not less.

CHAPTER TEN

Wet snowfalls, bare trees, coal shortages. The winter sky always veiled in gray. All merriment had gone from their lives. A new neighbor moved into the building. She was a Christian lady who was married to a Jewish man. Her name was Maya Goudsmit and she had a soft spot for Gabi, but also liked Hannah, and always made a point of saying hello and being friendly when Hannah met her in the back garden.

Without transportation, going to the dentist became an ordeal. If Hannah hadn't been wearing braces at night that needed to be checked she wouldn't have gone at all. Setting out after school, she had to walk very far south. When she arrived, the dentist, a Christian, felt sorry for her and gave her something to drink. Anne Frank had gone to the same dentist, and often Hannah and Anne had gone together to this scary, faraway place.

After seeing the dentist, it was pitch-black outside because it got dark so early in winter. The long walk home was even worse and when she got home she was scared and frozen.

As feared, one day the dreaded knock was heard at their own door. The soldiers were going house to house while loudspeakers on trucks in the street called for Jews to leave their apartments and assemble in the street at once. Without a moment to think, Hannah, Gabi, Mr. Goslar, Grandfather, Grandmother, and Irma were escorted from their building into a streetcar.

The streetcar passed tall, seventeenth-century canal houses in an older part of the city. Mist rose up from the canals. Rows of narrow, gabled houses leaned haphazardly against each other. There were signs barring Jews along the way, on shops, on benches. The shopping street was no longer crowded because there was less and less to buy. The Royal Palace was empty since the queen was in exile.

On the canals, good-looking young men pushed barges piled high with coal. They'd stand on the barges and push with long poles. They used to wink at the pretty schoolgirls who passed by, but no more because they too were cold and feeling the food shortages.

The Goslar family was taken to a theater in the

old Jewish Quarter near the zoo. The theater was named the Dutch Theater but, because it was now being used as an assembly point for Jews, they called it the Jewish Theater. Hundreds of people crowded into it in various states of terror.

Soldiers guarded them with rifles. After being marched past an officer at a table and having their papers examined, the Goslars were told to go home. But when they turned to leave, a soldier put his hand on Irma's shoulder and ordered that she remain behind.

Mr. Goslar tried to convince the official to let Irma leave with them, but he was rudely brushed off. Irma began to cry and plead but she was pushed into a group of prisoners being assembled. She was wearing the dress that Hannah's mother had given her for Hanukkah.

Of course Irma didn't know that it was a gift from Mrs. Goslar. Every year Mrs. Goslar told Irma to go to the seamstress. The seamstress would show Irma a dress and tell her it just happened to be Irma's size. She would give it to Irma and tell her that it had been made in the wrong size, that Irma could have it. Because Irma was simple, she never figured out that this was Mrs. Goslar's way of giving her a gift.

As Irma was restrained by the soldier with a rifle, the look on her face told them that as simple as she was, she knew exactly what was happening.

❧

After Easter, 1943, Hannah stopped going to school. Even though she was only fourteen she had to help with Gabi. Papa showed her how to do Mama's job in the kitchen. He showed her how to light the candles on the Sabbath. Her family lived in fear of what was to come. They had almost no money, and very little food to eat. But at least they were together.

On June 20, 1943, before it was light, there was a banging on their door. Then the bell was insistently rung. "Are there Jews living here?" a voice shouted in German.

Mr. Goslar went to the door. "*Ja*. There are Jews here," he answered also in German.

"You have twenty minutes! You may take twenty kilos only! Go down to the street! And hurry!" the Nazi soldier ordered, going on to the next door, where Hannah's grandparents lived, banging, and shouting, "Are there Jews living here?"

Hannah's rucksack had been packed and ready for months. She'd packed it herself, because she had no mother now, and Anne's mother—who would have helped her—was gone, too. Sanne's mother had helped her pack items that were of special necessity to growing girls.

Hannah felt like she was going to keel over. Her scrapbook was lying on the table. Also her Hebrew study books. Her father's briefcase was on the table, Gabi's toys were on the floor, and scholarly books were on a shelf. The room looked like Anne's had looked when Anne ran away, like someone was coming right back.

Outside in the street, the bridges had been pulled up. The entire neighborhood was sealed off by soldiers with weapons. There were trucks and motorcycles lined up. Hannah, her father, Gabi, and her grandparents stood close together. Tremors ran up and down Hannah's legs. Her heart was pounding. More and more people were assembling in the street, until it seemed as though every Jewish person in South Amsterdam was being roughly pushed into lines.

There were hundreds of people, whole families, old and sick people. There were single people whose relatives had already been taken. Each person, with a suitcase or a rucksack, was in terrible fear. A boy was so white, so scared, his parents had to hold him up.

The new neighbor, Maya Goudsmit, came hurrying toward them. She held her coat around her shoulders, some of her nightgown hanging down below the coat. She looked pleadingly at a soldier and begged him, "Can I take this little girl named Gabi and keep her?"

The soldier sneered at her, then raised his voice. "As a Dutch Christian, aren't you ashamed? The child is Jewish!"

There were shouts coming from loudspeakers saying, "Quickly! Begin to march toward the trucks! Quickly! Quickly! *Schnell!*"

The woman shouted back at the soldier, "I'm a Christian, a German Christian. And I am not ashamed!"

The assembled horde of Jewish people moved in rows. Mr. Goslar hoisted Gabi higher with one arm and gripped Hannah around her shoulders with the other arm. Her grandparents clasped each other's hands and walked, standing straight.

When Mr. Goslar and his family began to walk, Maya Goudsmit turned chalk-white and fainted.

CHAPTER ELEVEN

They were taken by truck to the Central Railway Station. Then they were loaded into cattle cars. Before the train began to move, the door was shut and the air quickly became stifling. The train went east. The new prisoners were going toward the German border. After traveling for several hours, the train stopped before crossing the dreaded border.

The door was opened by guards in green uniforms and the new prisoners saw barbed wire. Outside the fence were spruce trees and shrubs. Inside the fence was the mud and mosquito-infested transit camp called Westerbork. It was in Drente in eastern Holland.

Hannah's family were made to stand in line on the train platform for a very long time. When their turn came, her father and grandfather were instructed to go to one of the men's barracks. Mr. Goslar handed Gabi to Hannah and kissed his children before he was pushed along. Then her grandmother was moved away with all the women.

Gabi didn't cry but held on to Hannah. Fierce anxiety filled Hannah when her father, grandfather, and grandmother were marched away. Her heart froze. She kept her eyes glued on her father as his head bobbed above the other heads because he was so tall.

Only young children and a few girls her age were left on the platform. Everyone was distraught. Hannah, Gabi, and the other children were then led along a street by guards through the gluelike mud. Their luggage was stacked into wheelbarrows that were pulled along by men in brown overalls.

They were taken along another street to the orphanage that was a wooden barrack. There must have been seventy-five barracks in the camp and the train tracks went through the entire camp.

Inside the building into which they were led were dozens of children. Hannah was given a bowl and a mug. Then she and Gabi were assigned narrow little beds. The beds were two-tiered bunk beds. The thin mattresses were made of wood shavings that were covered with burlap. Because it was late they had missed the evening meal, but Hannah didn't feel hungry.

When they crawled into the hard beds, fleas began to bite. Hannah longed for her mother. But her mother was dead. She longed for her father or her grandmother and grandfather. She prayed that her father and grandmother and grandfather be protected, and for Alfred and Anne wherever they were.

In the morning after being taken to the washroom, Hannah was shown how to make her bed according to regulations. Then she and the other children went to a room with long benches. A trolley brought a warm drink like weak coffee for the adults and milk for the children, also chunks of bread. By now she was very hungry and she and Gabi ate every crumb.

Very quickly Hannah figured out where the men's barracks was in relation to the orphanage. When she learned that she would be given a work assignment, she volunteered to clean the toilets. She received baggy blue overalls to wear for this work detail. Someone asked her, "Why volunteer for such a disgusting task when you can volunteer to shell peas or work in the vegetable garden?"

The reason was that Hannah knew the washroom and toilets were close to the fence that separated them from the men's barracks. She hoped she could catch a glimpse of her father while she worked.

And her gamble proved correct. No sooner

had she gone with a scrub brush and bucket to the toilets and started to scrub the filthy zinc troughs than she saw her father pass. She ran out and, for a few moments, they were able to speak together across the fence.

This way, two or three times a day, she'd see him. Sometimes she could speak with him. She always felt much better after she had had a glimpse of her father. Sometimes she also had a glimpse of Grandfather and Grandmother.

Almost immediately she received a package from Maya Goudsmit. Inside was some food and a book about Florence Nightingale, the famous nurse.

Quickly the weather got very hot. The muddy road dried up, leaving fine dirt mixed with sand that coated everything in powdered, gray dust. Mosquitoes bred in the nearby swamp and, in swarms, infested the entire camp during the long summer. Between the mosquitoes and fleas, she and all the children were covered with itchy, red bites.

CHAPTER TWELVE

At Westerbork the entire camp lived in dread of Monday and Thursday nights. The tension built all day, and by evening everyone was in a state of hysteria. On Monday and Thursday nights the camp police came to each barrack. They read out the names of the people who were scheduled to be transported out of Westerbork the following day.

They heard the names: Auschwitz in Poland, Bergen-Belsen in Germany, Sobibor in Poland. These were the names of concentration camps where transports were going. While Westerbork was a transit camp only, rumors were that the other camps were for slave labor. The whispers were that conditions in these camps were much more brutal. Also that children, women, and those too weak to work often died.

"Because we have our Palestine document as well as our Paraguayan passports, we'll be safe," Mr. Goslar assured her.

So, on Monday and Thursday nights, after the

lists were read by the camp policeman in a green uniform, those whose names were called were terribly anxious. They would pack their scant possessions and would often weep all night with the knowledge that they would be transported into the unknown the next day. Perhaps they would even be gassed.

First thing on Tuesday and Friday mornings, those on the lists were marched to the train platform and loaded onto waiting cattle cars by SS men. Their belongings were piled high on carts. Throughout the camp could be heard the piercing sound of the train whistle. Then the noise of the train's engine as it creaked out of the station.

Most people in these trains were never heard from again.

With autumn came the cool, wet weather. Except for a sweater or two Hannah and Gabi had almost nothing for winter in their rucksacks. I'm so dumb, Hannah thought. The damp went right through their skimpy clothes.

With the rains, the street turned once again into sticky mud. The prisoners called the largest street the Boulevard des Misery. If Hannah wasn't careful, her shoes would get stuck in the goo. It rained and stormed so much that black and green mold coated the walls of the barracks.

Between her work detail at the toilets and helping with the younger children at the orphanage, Hannah was busy all day. She was glad. This meant she was not alone. In groups there was at least a feeling of camaraderie, as if they were all survivors of a shipwreck, together in a lifeboat. Granted it was a squalid lifeboat, but it was afloat nonetheless and filled with Jewish spirit.

After they'd been in Westerbork for two weeks, Gabi cried the entire night. Hannah didn't know what to do when Gabi wouldn't stop crying. In the morning she felt Gabi's forehead. She was burning with fever. Shivers made Gabi's body shake. Her eyes were red and angry, her nose oozing.

Gabi put her hands over both ears. She scrunched up her purple face and continued to bellow. Nothing would calm her. Hannah realized that something was very wrong. Every time Hannah tried to touch her little sister, Gabi pushed her hands away and screamed louder. Finally Hannah scooped up the little girl and carried her to the vast hospital barrack.

Immediately doctors, who were also Jewish prisoners, operated on Gabi's ears.

After work, Hannah went to the hospital.

When she got there, her father and grandparents were standing at Gabi's bed.

From then on they were able to be together at Gabi's bedside. A huge bandage was wrapped around Gabi's head and ears. She was very ill. Her eyes were shiny with anger and tears but she was no longer screaming. Mr. Goslar tried to get her to eat but she wouldn't. Hannah tried but couldn't get her to eat, either.

In the evening the sound of airplane engines were heard high in the sky. Much later, in the middle of the night, more airplane engines were heard. At night in the eastern part of the sky was the Little Dipper constellation. As the night passed, the constellation would climb and begin to cross the sky. On the opposite side of the sky was the constellation of the Lion. Wherever Anne and Alfred were, were these same constellations crossing the sky?

❦

In November a rumor spread rapidly through the camp. It was that the Nazis would no longer respect any special lists and that, from then on, those on lists would be deported, too. In a panic Hannah hung around trying to catch a glimpse of her father. She could not find him.

After the dinner of turnips and moldy bread, a camp policeman came to the orphanage. He announced that the Palestine lists had been invalidated and that everyone on these lists would be transported to the East for resettlement. After shuffling though papers he added that only the names on the first two lists were still valid.

Because of Mr. Goslar's high position back in Germany before the war, her family had been put on the second list. As soon as the police had gone, Hannah ran down the road to the hospital. There, leaning down and talking softly to Gabi, stood Papa. Gabi was eating a small tomato.

"The Palestine lists are invalidated," Hannah told him.

He told her he already knew.

"Except for the first list and the second. And we're on the second. Right?"

She had to make sure.

"Yes, Hanneli, we're on the second list. We are spared this time." He told her that though they were spared they must pray for those who would have to go on the transports the next day.

The next day, the unusually large transport of one thousand people left. Afterwards the camp was subdued.

Then, more trains arrived from Amsterdam

bringing newly arrested people to Westerbork. Rain fell from the gray sky, soaking the ugly barracks, the wooden watchtowers, the S or punishment barracks.

Those who had committed some crime against the Nazis were kept in the S barracks. These so-called "criminals" had tried to run away, or had been discovered in hiding places. Some had joined the anti-Nazi underground movement to either sabotage the Nazis or aid those in need of help.

These "criminals" from S barracks stood out. A red patch was sewn onto their overalls. The men were shaved bald and were made to wear caps. The women's hair was cropped short. Because they were given much less food, people from S barracks were hungrier than everyone else. Because they were given no soap, they were very dirty. Often vermin infested their clothes.

The rain continued to fall. When it stopped, the temperature dropped. Ice formed, making it very slippery to walk. Because Hannah had nothing but a sweater, there was no way to get away from the dampness and cold, inside or out.

CHAPTER THIRTEEN

Because of the cold, everything froze in the toilets and washrooms, making Hannah's work very hard. Her hands were chafed and raw from scrubbing, and from the harsh disinfectant. The wind irritated her eyes. Icy rain and sleet fell all the time.

Every day, after she finished her work, she rushed to the hospital to see Gabi. Thankfully the doctors who had operated on her ears had been skilled. It was hard to see her little face beneath the big bandage. When Hannah or her father or grandparents appeared at her bedside, Gabi reached up her little hands to be picked up. But Gabi was beginning to speak and chatter again.

After seeing her family, Hannah would hurry back to the orphanage through the icy streets. She deftly lifted her shoes to keep from slipping.

In the evening Hannah and other older girls helped with the small children in the orphanage. The big girls helped feed them, wash their clothes, change the soiled rags that were being used as diapers, cuddle them, play games, and sing songs with them. They taught them the little songs that Dutch children liked to sing.

One song went:

Kling klang het klotje

It was about a clock.

Another song went:

Constant had een hobbelpaad,

Zonder kop of zonder staart

This was a song about a hobbyhorse with no head and no tail. It made the children laugh.

Hearing the children's voices, Hannah remembered a song Anne's father had taught them when they were very little. It went:

Jo di wi di wo di wi di waya, katschkaja,

Katschko, di wi di wo di,

wi di witsch witsch witsch bum!

Ying jang, jing jang bums kada witschki

Yank kai wi di wi, Yang kai wi di wi

Jing jang jing jang! Bums kada witsche

Jang kai wi di wi. Ajah!

Hanneli and Anne had sung this song constantly when very young. It was their song; no one else knew it. Mr. Frank had told them that the song was Chinese, and they had believed him. Of course later they realized that he'd been kidding and the words meant nothing, but neither of them ever forgot their song.

❧

Hanneli remembered the very first time she and Anne had set eyes on each other in 1933. Their mothers were shopping for groceries in a neighborhood shop in South Amsterdam. Being new arrivals from Germany they started speaking in German to each other. Little Anne and little Hannah had eyed each other. Neither had said hello. Anne had big eyes and was looking around at everything, curiously. Hannah had naturally lustrous hair, very creamy skin, was shy but very huggable.

On the very first day at the Montessori school, Mrs. Goslar had had to drag Hannah to the door of the kindergarten class. Because Hannah couldn't speak the Dutch language, she didn't want to go to school. She sobbed and resisted the entire way.

At the door to the classroom Hannah clutched her mother's dress, refusing to let go. Through her tears she saw a girl standing at the front of the classroom, playing the bells. The girl's back was to the door but when she turned around Hannah saw it was the same girl from the neighborhood shop. Her face was radiant; the bells made tingling noises.

The girl saw Hannah and smiled at her in a friendly way.

Hannah ran into her arms.

She forgot about her mother, forgot about being afraid. The girl was named Anneliese Marie, but everyone called her Anne. And, right away, Anne called her Hanneli instead of Hannah.

Of course that was so long ago. Lucky Anne was safe in Switzerland wearing warm clothes, together with her sister, her father, her mother, maybe even eating a real egg and buttered toast.

❧

Most of the children in the orphanage had gotten separated from their parents. Some had been put in hiding places by their parents but had been discovered. Others had been left by the Nazis when their parents were arrested. None of them had any idea what had become of their parents.

Many were infants who had been in Westerbork such a long time that it was doubtful they'd recognize their own parents if they saw them again. To a few of these little ones, Hannah became like a mother and they'd wait anxiously for her to come back from the hospital or from work.

For Hanukkah the older children in the barracks made a play for the younger ones. They based it on a poem called "The Diver," by the great German poet Friedrich von Schiller. It was the story of a king who challenges his knights to dive for a golden goblet that he has thrown deep into the dangerous sea. Because the sea is so tumultuous no knight dares to dive into it. Finally a simple boy dives into the whirlpool and—against all odds— emerges holding the goblet.

Curious as to what lies at the bottom of the sea, the king offers the boy a priceless stone, the rank of knight, and the princess's hand in marriage if the boy will dive down once again into the dangerous sea and tell him what is at the bottom. Though the princess begs him not to dive, the boy plunges back into the whirlpool.

In Schiller's poem, the youth drowns. But, for Hanukkah, the older children in the barracks at Westerbork changed the ending of the play. Their boy rises up from the wild sea with the goblet. He is knighted. He is rewarded. He and the princess are married, and all the children in the orphanage cheered.

CHAPTER FOURTEEN

One night, a woman told Hannah that her friend Sanne Ledermann had been arrested and had just arrived at Westerbork.

The next day, Hannah saw an arm waving in quick flagging motions. She looked as hard as she could. Yes, of course, it was Sanne. It couldn't have been anyone else. How wonderful! That day they were able to say a few words to each other. Sometimes Hannah passed a factory where women from S barracks sat at long tables and broke old batteries down into parts. Nearby the factory she saw Sanne in a women's work group.

How grown-up Sanne was looking. Sanne was starting to look more like a woman than a teenage girl. Then Hannah thought, What about Anne, so far away? And was Ilse safe wherever she was? Would Jacque continue to be safe? Sanne had no news of Jacque, but because Jacque was only half Jewish she must be safe in Amsterdam.

They were all growing up without each other. Maybe they wouldn't even recognize each other after the war. Hannah occasionally saw Sanne until Sanne and her parents were sent to Auschwitz in November.

Also in November Hannah's grandfather suddenly died of a heart attack. She felt sick with sadness.

It rained all the time. On the last Monday in November a camp policeman came into the barracks to read the lists for the usual Tuesday transports. He began to read the names. Hannah heard gasps because the names being read were the names of the children in the orphanage. She held her breath as he read off name after name after name. The time has come, she thought.

She listened but did not hear her own name.

He finished explaining that all must prepare their things and be ready to leave on the morning transport. Hannah wanted to shout, You idiot, can't you see these are helpless little children? What can you do with them?

The policeman turned away and opened the door. Outside, the rain kept falling from the pitch-black sky, heavier than before. The policeman stepped into the swirling silvery drops, and vanished with his terrible list.

The orphanage was in turmoil. Looking around, Hannah realized that, except for hers and a few others', every child's name had been read. Though they had thought the children would be safe here, the entire orphanage was about to be emptied.

Word must have traveled through the camp, because quickly several of the teachers and Rabbi Vorst rushed into the barracks. They tried to calm the children and each other. They all knew the terrible rumors of the harsh treatment of young children and old people in the concentration camps to the East.

Through the night Hannah comforted the frightened children. In the first light she helped them pack their meager things into bundles. Her favorites clung to her neck, aware that something terrible was about to happen.

In the morning, Rabbi Vorst returned to the orphanage. He spread his large, frayed, blue-and-white prayer shawl with its long fringes over the heads of all the children. Gravely—with tears streaming across his cheeks and into his beard—he blessed them.

Hannah covered her face with her hands and cried.

When the time came to march the children to the trains, their teachers arrived at the orphanage with their own belongings. Though the teachers weren't on the lists, they had decided it was their duty to accompany the children. They would go with the children onto the trains and share whatever fate had waiting.

Hannah hoisted up two little ones and also their bags. The rain had stopped and cold sun glared down. She walked with the children. The older children marched in rows of three toward the trains. As they walked, Hannah felt cold in every part of her being.

A guard shouted at her to stop and go no further. Reluctantly she handed her little ones over to a teacher. She couldn't watch any longer and walked back to the almost empty orphanage. Her shoes stuck to the icy mud and she could hear the children's voices singing. Their voices were so sweet, so warm against the cruelty and cold.

It was eerie in the orphanage because all the children were gone. The next morning it was a relief to go off to work in the frozen toilets.

CHAPTER FIFTEEN

On an evening in January of the new year, 1944, Mr. Goslar approached Gabi's hospital bed. Hannah was feeding Gabi. She looked up and saw a light in his eyes. "Good news!" he told her. He explained that shortly they would all be transported to another place. Together.

Hannah wanted to know since when was any transport good news? Her tone was impudent. She wondered if she was becoming more outspoken and bold like Anne Frank used to be. Mr. Goslar explained that they'd been put on a list that was going to go to a concentration camp in Germany. It was called Bergen-Belsen. The rumor was that Bergen-Belsen was an exchange camp, not a work camp.

He told her that because of their Paraguayan passports, and the fact that they were on the remaining Palestine lists, that they were of special value to the Nazis and the Nazis were putting them in an exchange camp. That way they could be used to exchange for German prisoners of war. They were like pieces in a chess game.

Now Hannah, too, felt exhilarated and asked when would they go? He told her that it would be soon.

And it was. On the night of February 14, Hannah heard her name and Gabi's read out by the camp policeman. That night she packed her rucksack, filling it with their clothes. All their things were shabby, dirty, outgrown. Stupid summer clothes, she thought, as she folded the dresses and blouses that she'd kept as clean as she'd been able to with very little soap.

On the morning of February 14, she and her father and grandmother stood on the train platform. Mr. Goslar had gotten Gabi released from the hospital early in the morning. He held her in his arms. Hannah carried their rucksack. Gabi's ears were still swathed in big bandages. The bandages were not very clean and smelled of pus. Gabi was looking at everything with big eyes. She spoke rapidly. "Papa. Hanneli. Grandma. Train. Soup."

On the platform the large group to be transported gathered and the guards put them into lines of five. Rather than the usual cattle cars used in transports to Auschwitz, they were given passenger cars. Hannah recognized some of the faces on the platform. All had one special passport or another or were on special lists.

The SS guard put red stamps on their papers, then shouted, "*Schnell!* Hurry!"

Roughly they were pushed aboard the train. Mr. Goslar, Hannah, Gabi, and Grandmother were squeezed into the same compartment that already held several others. Then the doors were shoved closed and bolted shut.

For two days the bad smell of Gabi's puss-filled bandages filled the compartment as the train traveled. The shades had been lowered so they could not see outside. Though they did not know if it was day or night, they knew that the train was taking them to the dreaded East. For two days only a little bread and a small amount of water was distributed.

Gabi kept asking for food, but they had very little to give her as the train stopped and started many times. It slowed, passed a platform, but didn't stop. Finally the train stopped. The compartment door was pulled open. It was daytime. A loudspeaker barked out that they should take all their belongings with them and disembark. They were ordered, "Walk quickly. *Schnell!* Line up."

They did as ordered.

Hannah's first sight when her feet touched ground was that they were in the middle of nowhere. A line of SS men stood shoulder to shoulder holding grizzled German shepherd dogs on leather leashes in one hand and whips in the other hand. In their holsters were pistols.

The dogs were very large and had yellow eyes. They were straining on their leashes. Hannah hesitated, afraid to pass close to the dogs. Mr. Goslar and Grandmother knew she was afraid of dogs and tried to shield her, but it was impossible to avoid the snarling faces of the dogs when she was pushed along. The breath of the dreaded dogs came out like steam in the cold air.

Their entire trainload of people was marched away from the empty train by the soldiers with dogs. They were taken along a snowy road, through a snow-covered field, passing bare willow trees.

Hannah felt dizzy from lack of food. Mr. Goslar was weak, too, and was having a hard time keeping up. Tall rolls of barbed wire fenced the field. The barren field stretched on and on. In the distance were watchtowers, barracks, more barbed wire. This was Bergen-Belsen on the Lüneburg Heath in Germany.

They were told to stop, and Hannah and Gabi were grouped with mothers and children and were put in a truck. Her father and grandmother were left with the others. Hannah was overwhelmed with panic as the truck that she was in drove past her father and grandmother and the long line of marching men and women.

The truck passed what seemed to be a series of smaller camps within the larger camp until it entered a new camp that was called Alballalager. The truck halted and the mothers and children were told, "Climb down. Line up."

The prisoners were counted, then immediately recounted. Where had they taken her father and grandmother? Hannah asked this question of a woman who was leading her group but who seemed to be Jewish.

"They are being taken to be deloused and quarantined. Don't worry. You'll see them after that."

This woman told Hannah that Alballalager was a privileged camp, that her clothes wouldn't be taken, that her hair wouldn't be shaved, that her family wouldn't be separated, that numbers wouldn't be tattooed on their arms. The woman told Hannah that she was very lucky indeed. She pointed toward the other camps beyond their barbed-wire fence, grimaced, and let the pupils of her eyes roll up toward the heavens.

CHAPTER SIXTEEN

Hannah and Gabi were put into a barracks. A group of Greek prisoners, who had been there a long time, had taken charge. Though they were Jewish, too, they kept the camp running for their Nazi bosses. Some of these people were kind to the new arrivals, but some were not.

Hannah and Gabi were assigned lower bunks that were side by side. Each bed was a thin slab covered with straw. Hannah had become like a mother to Gabi. Every night she stretched a skimpy blanket over Gabi, and one over herself. She doubted if Gabi even remembered their mother at all by now. But Hannah remembered her and always would. And she also remembered her friends Anne, Sanne, Ilse, Jacque. She remembered Alfred and Grandpa.

Gabi was very weak. Though everyone under age three got two glasses of milk, because Gabi was three and a half she didn't get any. Gabi got weaker and weaker until the wife of the rabbi from

Salonika, Greece, began to give Gabi two glasses of milk each week. Two glasses of milk could make the difference between life and death. Hannah reminded this woman that she could give her nothing in return for the milk and that she could easily have sold or traded her milk ration for other food or clothes, or given it to her own children. The rabbi's wife insisted that it was her right to do what she pleased with her milk.

After this, Gabi began to get well.

The barracks were colder than the Westerbork barracks had been. In fact, Bergen-Belsen was much colder than Westerbork. The dampness was worse, too. At dawn, Hannah felt sick to her stomach. When she sat up things began to swim before her eyes; a hum filled her ears. She started to vomit.

She felt terribly ill indeed. She couldn't get out of bed. A racking cough began. Every few minutes she had to vomit. She was frightened, because she had to care for Gabi.

Six A.M. was the time of roll call. To miss roll call was to be shot. Dizzily she climbed down from the bed. She went outside with the other women and stood in a row of five between two women who bolstered her up until they were counted by the Nazi guards. She wanted to faint, was shivering uncontrollably, but held on until they returned to the barracks to wait for the morning meal.

An old woman asked if she knew that her skin was yellow. Hannah hadn't known that. Yellow skin meant jaundice, a dangerous illness from poor sanitation. Hannah had seen many women with yellow faces carted off to the hospital. Some had never returned. This explained her awful symptoms.

She began to cry. What could she do? There was no one else to take care of her sister. She tried to keep going. The food came. It was all she could do to hold Gabi's bowl out to be filled. "Hanneli sick?" Gabi asked.

Hannah didn't care whether or not the chunk of bread and dollop of margarine were put in her own bowl. The last thing on her mind was food. Involuntarily her eyes shut and she saw spots in front of her. She felt worse than she'd felt in her entire life. I must go to the hospital, she thought, but I can't leave Gabi. Oh God, tell me what to do?

She felt a cool hand on her forehead. She opened her eyes and saw a tall woman standing beside the older woman who had spoken to her earlier.

"This is my niece," said the old woman.

"I'm Mrs. Abrahams," the tall woman explained. "I'll care for your little sister. You must go to the hospital!"

Hannah wondered what her father would want her to do.

The old lady explained that her niece, Mrs. Abrahams, had seven children and Gabi would be part of the family. Mrs. Abrahams had five daughters with her, and Mr. Abrahams had their two sons with him in another barrack. "When you get out of hospital, we would also like you to join our family."

"But why?" asked Hannah emotionally, knowing what a kind offer was being made.

Mrs. Abrahams took Hannah's hot hand in her own cool hand. She gently massaged the pulse on the wrist. "I know your father. He helps everybody."

Hannah's head was swimming again. The nausea was back. She pushed Gabi into Mrs. Abrahams's arms.

"Go to the hospital first thing tomorrow morning, Hanneli. Get well. And when you are well, come to me. We'll be one family."

CHAPTER SEVENTEEN

For more than a month Hannah lay in the hospital. She was too sick to notice much, except that her father and grandmother sat with her whenever they could. Someone tried to get her to drink. She understood the gestures but not the words because the voice was speaking to her in Greek. The blanket smelled like disinfectant and all around were groans and sighs, the sound of pouring rain, of shouted orders in the distance.

When she opened her eyes at last, her father was sitting beside her. Had she been delirious for a long time? He told her she had. She was so weak that the enamel food bowl was too heavy to lift. When her father walked away from the bed, from the back he looked like a grandfather instead of a father, he had aged so.

As she lay there, rains fell incessantly, also snow. When it was neither raining nor snowing, the sky was steely and gray.

At last she was ordered back to her barracks.

She walked on wobbly legs. Across the barbed wire she could see dead bodies waiting for burial laid out in piles like logs. Hannah kept her eyes to the ground hoping to keep from looking at dead bodies in piles or thrown into pits.

Gabi was so happy to see her and threw her arms around Hannah's neck. The smelly bandages had been removed from Gabi's ears and Gabi's hair had grown. Mrs. Abrahams had indeed cared for Gabi and had even secured a bed for Hannah in the section of the barracks where she and her five daughters were.

In spite of the food shortage, Hannah and Gabi had continued growing, and their clothes no longer fit properly. Though children under sixteen were not supposed to work, for a short time Hannah was assigned to a group of women at a cellophane bag factory. Every day after roll call, after bread and watery coffee, she walked to the factory. Along the way she got glimpses of the other camps.

Through the barbed wire were prisoners in zebra-striped pajamas with shaved heads. These people were in various states of malnourishment and disease. As bad as Alballalager was, having a Paraguayan passport and being on the Palestine list meant that at least they got a little food and water and lived in better conditions.

Hannah's factory made bags out of sheets of cellophane. She and a group of women stood all day twisting cellophane into braids, then wove the braids into carrier bags. Though their feet hurt from standing all day, the work was not difficult. They worked all morning. In the middle of the afternoon a large kettle was hoisted in by two or three women. Often the soup consisted of turnip pieces with a few bad potatoes on the bottom. Everyone watched very carefully to make sure that their soup was ladled from the bottom where the nourishment was, not the watery top of the kettle.

Mr. Goslar worked at a factory where military shoes were stacked in huge piles. These were shoes that soldiers had used in battle. They were mud-caked, worn down, twisted up and stiff from dry rot, blood, and rain. It was the prisoners' job to take the shoes apart with tools. Then—from the old parts—another group of prisoners chose the least damaged shoe parts and used them for replacements. In this way, recycled shoes were fashioned.

The work was very dirty and dusty. Also, the prisoners had a quota to meet every day that caused constant anxiety because the quota was almost impossible.

Mr. Goslar grew weaker all the time until the rabbi from Salonika, who Mr. Goslar knew from Berlin, had to help him get to work.

In May, due to malnourishment and overwork, Mr. Goslar was put into the special barracks where there were only sick people.

In July Grandmother was put on one of the lists for transfer. Instead of going, she went to the SS and told them to take her off the list. They thought she was crazy but did as she asked.

Why? people asked her. Why had she given up her chance to be transferred? The answer was that she couldn't leave her granddaughters. She would stay and help them if she could. Of course the truth was that there wasn't much she could do to help them, or anyone, but she remained in a barrack nearby.

One day while standing at roll call, Hannah saw, in what had been an empty field beside their camp, that large tents had been erected. Because more and more people were pouring off trains every day, all of the various sections of Bergen-Belsen were overflowing and now people would have to make do with tents. The existing camp sections couldn't hold all of these new arrivals, and new barracks were also under construction.

Often at roll call, when everyone had finally been counted, the guard would bark for the prisoners to stay where they were because they had to be recounted. These prisoners had already been standing for an hour, so this meant even more standing. Why must we count again? wondered Hannah.

Someone told her that the Germans wanted to make sure that no one had run away. Run away? But where could we run? Hannah thought angrily. Without money? With stars on our clothes? With nothing? In the middle of Germany?

CHAPTER EIGHTEEN

Time passed and again it was dark in the morning when the prisoners stood freezing at roll call. Everyone dressed and undressed in the dark. It got so cold in November that clothes were sometimes frozen solid, so cold that half of a sleeve might break off in someone's hand.

Hannah knew it was November, but didn't know the exact date. If it was the twelfth, it was her sixteenth birthday. But she didn't know for sure.

One day a terrible rain and windstorm blew all day. The wind was so strong that the women had to link arms with each other in order to walk. All day the wail of the wind against the flimsy planks of the factory walls could be heard.

When Hannah returned to her barracks in the evening, she saw in the distance that the huge tents were blowing into the air. The wind blew big gusts and suddenly the tents collapsed. There was a great commotion where the tents had blown down.

When Hannah entered her barracks Gabi rushed to meet her and wrapped her arms around Hannah's legs. Hannah bent down to hug Gabi. She pressed her frozen lips against Gabi's cheek. Despite the cold in the barracks, Gabi's cheek felt warm against Hannah's numb lips.

Gabi pointed out men in zebra-striped pajamas who were at work in their barracks. They were working on the wooden bunk beds. The wooden tables and benches were taken away.

A third bunk was added so now the bunks were stacked three high. When they finished, everyone pushed to claim a bed when hundreds of new inmates arrived. Where three hundred people had been housed, now were six hundred.

From then on, everyone shared a bed with someone else. Hannah and Gabi shared one narrow bed.

Outside, metal poles were placed in a line and barbed wire was suspended between the poles. Alballalager was divided down the middle into two cramped camps. New transports were arriving night and day and everyone in every camp was sleeping two in a bed, sometimes three.

The rumor was that Polish prisoners in poor condition who had been living in the tents were now living beside them. The barbed wire that divided the camp was covered with bunches of straw. Hannah could hear sounds made by the new arrivals, she could smell the filth, but the faces of the prisoners couldn't be seen at all through the thick layer of straw.

Of course, it was forbidden to speak to these people anyway.

All day and night guards with rifles looked at them from the watchtowers. The penalty for speaking across the wire was death. Death by shooting, or death by some other cruel means. Nonetheless, a few of the women in the barracks were curious about their new neighbors. At night they hung around near the barbed wire and straw fence trying to pick up a little news. But not Hannah. She never went near the fence.

At the same time that their camp was divided and crowded to the point of bursting, the food rations were cut down. Before, the food had been bad and meager, now there was almost none. Everyone talked of nothing but food. They could think of nothing else. Some people stole bread for the hungry children, but others stole from the children for themselves.

At night the prisoners stood close to the makeshift stove where a few bits of wood were burning and gave off a little heat. The talk always turned to food. Mrs. Abrahams confessed that she was thinking of soup, of chicken soup with fat matzoh balls.

Another woman dreamed about holiday cakes and cookies with powdered sugar sprinkled on top.

Gabi and the other small children didn't know what cookies and holiday cakes were, nor did they know what chicken was anymore. When someone tried to explain to the children what sugar tasted like it was hopeless because no one could find accurate enough words to describe the glorious taste of sugar or cookies or cakes.

Hannah dreamed of a big breakfast, the kind of breakfast she and Anne had had after a sleepover. First she dreamed of a warm bath, then breakfast in bed under a feather eiderdown. She would like an egg. She would like it to be boiled. She would like toast. The toast would be hot. Best of all the toast would be coated with thick, melting butter.

And hot coffee with real cream, Hannah thought, almost swooning.

CHAPTER NINETEEN

Hanukkah was coming and Mrs. Abrahams wanted to make a little something special for the children. Because there was so little food, everyone's head hurt, their joints and teeth ached. People often lost track of the days, were dizzy and weak, their thinking had gotten fuzzy.

Besides the terrible hunger, Hannah was constantly worried about her father. Since they'd cut the food rations, her father was becoming skeletal. His eyes were sunk into his skull while the rest of his face was swollen because of edema. Nonetheless he still sat in the sick barracks with dignity and spent his spare time giving encouragement to sick, old people.

People were dying in their beds or at roll call. Some simply sat down and couldn't get up again. Dead bodies were gathered up and tipped from stretchers into open pits. When Hannah passed near one of these stinking pits filled with corpses, she couldn't look. Hungry black birds flew and screeched above these pits all day long. She decided never to pass that part of the camp again.

In preparation for Hanukkah all Mrs. Abrahams could do was put aside a few scraps of food. Mrs. Abrahams's aunt worked in the kitchen and scrounged slices of fried potato and half a carrot. No one felt like celebrating anyway. So, little was said about the holiday they'd always called the Festival of Lights. The bits of food were shared and devoured with very little spirit until the makeshift Hanukkah candles that Mr. Goslar had made from drops of margarine were lighted. Then everyone sighed.

In the barracks, a woman told Hannah that though the rumor was that there were Polish and Hungarian people on the other side of the wire fence, she had heard that there were also Dutch women who had been transferred from Auschwitz in Poland. When Hannah heard that, she waited until it was nighttime, then headed toward the door. Someone reminded her that it was snowing. An-other warned her to avoid the searchlight and not to go near the fence.

She stole outside. The falling snow was heavy. Minute wet smears landed on her face and ears, white flakes tumbling out of the dark. She listened. Gusts of wind were blowing. She thought she heard muted voices speaking in Dutch. But then the wind gusted, drowning out the faint voices. She strained to listen as the searchlight swept across the barracks, then disappeared around a corner.

When the wind died down at last, Hannah pricked up her ears again. Instead of the Dutch language she could hear a woman singing a raucous holiday song in Czech. I must have been mistaken, she thought. I only imagined I heard Dutch voices.

She went back inside and lay on her hard bed beside Gabi. She fell asleep thinking vividly about food.

Hannah (circled, left) and Anne (circled, right) in their classroom. Amsterdam, 1935.

Hannah and her father. Amsterdam, 1936.

Hannah and her mother on the Merwedeplein in front of their building. Amsterdam, 1936.

Friends in a sandbox, July 1937. Hannah is at far left; Anne is second from left.

Anne (left) and Hannah (right) in front of their building, May 1939.

Anne Frank's birthday party, June 1939. Anne is second from left; Hannah is fourth from left.

Hannah and her grandfather. Amsterdam, 1941.

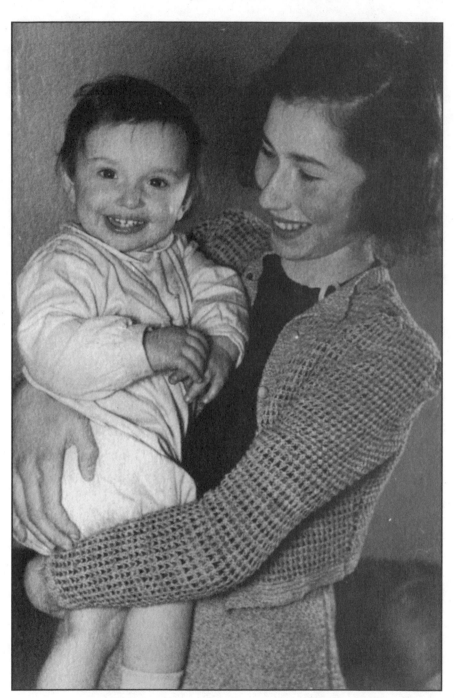

Hannah (right) and Gabi (left). Amsterdam, 1942.

Ration coupons, 1943.

Gabi, at about age fifteen.

Hannah, her grandchildren, and her daughter, Ruth. Israel, 1994.

CHAPTER TWENTY

The year 1945 began with bitter cold. The whispers were that the Germans were losing the war. These were the whispers but no one had any proof. The Nazi guards were as cruel as ever. Airplanes flew over their heads day and night. Nothing except these whispers gave any indication that their oppressors might lose the war.

Could it be true? Hannah wondered. Would it be too late? How much longer could Papa last? How much longer could she and Gabi or any of them last?

One afternoon while Hannah was at the factory, an explosion was heard near her father's barracks. A fighter plane had dropped several bombs and part of the barracks was hit directly. Later Mr. Goslar told her that luckily everyone but one man was outside. This man had been praying at one end of the barracks nowhere near his bunk. When the bomb hit only one bunk was destroyed. It was that man's bunk. Had he been in bed, he would have died.

Mr. Goslar was very sick. His face looked like it was made of wax. Like most of the men in the camp, his clothes were threadbare and dirty. He would touch his daughters' cheeks and assure them that any day now they would be among those exchanged for German prisoners. When he saw Hannah's skeptical look he urged her not to lose faith.

A very short time later a man came to the factory to tell Hannah that her father had been put in the hospital. When she went to see him he was sleeping. She looked at his gray face with apprehension.

❧

When February came Hannah had been in Bergen-Belsen a year. After work she would bend over the stove toward the small bit of heat and stretch her purple, frozen hands. When she had rubbed at the numbness, the sharp sting of pins and needles hurt her hands.

Mrs. Abrahams told Hannah that she had been right, there were Dutch people on the other side of the fence. In fact, a woman there said that there was someone who knew Hannah.

Hannah summoned up her courage to risk the danger and, when it was dark, scurried over to the fence. Her breath billowed out in front of her. She prayed that the guard would not notice her there, that the searchlight would not pass across her. Am I crazy to risk everything by doing this? she asked herself and answered yes. But having human contact with someone Dutch would mean a great deal.

In Dutch she whispered softly into the barbed wire and straw.

A voice whispered back in Dutch. "Who are you?"

Hannah heard movement but could see nothing through the straw.

"It's Hannah Goslar from South Amsterdam."

She heard the voice say in Dutch, "Hanneli Goslar, it's me, Mrs. van Daan, the friend of the Frank family."

Hannah remembered Mrs. van Daan slightly. Her husband had worked with Mr. Frank at his office. Sometimes when her parents went to the Frank house for coffee and cake on Sunday afternoon, the van Daans and their son Peter had been among the guests.

"Do you know that your friend Anne is here?" Mrs. van Daan asked her.

Hannah couldn't have heard her right.

"Anne is in Switzerland."

"No. She's here. Do you want me to get her?" Mrs. van Daan asked.

"Oh! Yes!"

"I can't get Margot, she's very sick, but I'll get Anne."

Hannah prayed that the guard would not pass by. Her heart was pounding with elation. How could this be possible? She waited, excited but fearful all at once.

"Hanneli? Is it really you?"

Of course it was Anne's voice.

"It's me! I'm here."

They began to cry.

"What are you doing here? You're supposed to be in Switzerland." Hannah asked.

Anne quickly told her that Switzerland was a ruse, that they had wanted the Nazis to think they had fled to Switzerland, but really her family had gone into hiding.

Anne explained that they'd been hiding the whole time in a storage annex behind Mr. Frank's office on Prinsengracht. She told her that Miep Gies, who was their friend and also worked for Otto Frank, and a few others employees of her father, had looked after them for twenty-five months until they were arrested and deported.

For two years Anne had never stepped outside the hiding place, had not been allowed to write letters or contact anyone. They had had food and clothes. They were warm. It seemed like they would survive because the war was coming to an end, the Germans were losing.

Astonished, Hannah asked Anne if she knew for sure that the Germans were losing.

Anne assured her that it was true. Because they had had a radio in hiding, she was sure. On June 6, 1944, the Americans and British and Canadians had landed in France and had begun beating back the Germans. At the same time, in the East, the Russians had been pushing the Germans back. Then she told Hannah that her group in hiding were arrested in August and put in jail. Her family was sent to S barracks in Westerbork. In Westerbork Anne had worked at the battery factory.

Hannah told Anne that she had been in Westerbork, too. Hannah remembered the shaved heads in S barracks in Westerbork. She remembered looking into the battery factory and seeing women at work. She realized that if Anne was much more grown up, she must be, too. It had been nearly two years since she'd seen herself in a mirror. Anne said Westerbork was hard but at least her family had been together.

Then, Anne told her emotionally, they were transported to Auschwitz, her father was taken away with the other men, things had gone from bad to worse for them since then. When she and Margot were shipped to Bergen-Belsen their mother had not been sent with them. She and Margot feared the worst for their parents. There were gas chambers in Auschwitz, Anne told her; night and day thousands of people were gassed and cremated.

Hannah was stunned by this information. Could it be possible? It must be; Anne had seen it with her own eyes.

Anne asked urgently about Hannah's parents.

Hannah told her that Mrs. Goslar had died in Amsterdam before they were arrested. So had the new baby. Grandfather had died in Westerbork. She explained that so far the rest of her family had managed to stay together—Gabi with her, Papa and Grandmother, all in the same camp but in different barracks. But now, she told Anne desolately, her father was in the hospital. He was very, very sick.

"You're so lucky to have your family. I don't have parents anymore, Hanneli. I have nobody. Margot is very sick, too."

Again they began crying.

"They shaved my head."

Hannah thought, How terrible for Anne, she was so proud of her thick, lustrous hair.

The searchlight from the watchtower swept through the dark night. Hannah thought, Anne's not the same person. Neither am I. We're broken girls.

Desperately Anne revealed that she and Margot didn't have anything at all to eat in their compound. They were frozen and Margot was very sick. They'd been living in tents, but these had blown down. She also confided that they didn't have any wearable clothes since lice were in everything.

Hannah thought, Maybe I can scrounge up something for them. At least we have a little!

She asked Anne to meet her on the following night.

Anne reminded her how dangerous it was to talk to her, but said she would try to meet Hannah again.

CHAPTER TWENTY-ONE

Lying beside Gabi, Hannah thought about the improbability of her reunion with Anne. She thanked God. Of course it was terrible that Anne was here and not in Switzerland. Hannah could barely believe what had actually just happened. When she thought over Anne's information that the war was coming to an end, that the Germans were losing, her spirits rose. Dare I hope that we will all go home? That Anne and I will walk to school together, maybe even this spring? she thought.

Her heart hammered with this miraculous possibility.

At age four, when they couldn't speak Dutch yet and wore little flowered dresses, Hannah and Anne had walked to school in the morning and home in the afternoon. At eight they'd ridden bicycles, at ten they'd gone swimming in summer and skating in winter, at twelve they'd played Ping-Pong and talked about the goings-on between boys and girls.

Once for Purim, Mr. Goslar had gotten dressed up as Hitler, painted a little whisk-broom mustache onto his lip, and knocked at the Franks' door. The sight of Hitler had given them all a fright, then a big laugh.

On the day of Anne's last birthday, the twelfth of June in 1942, Hannah had kissed her parents and hurried down the street. It was Anne's thirteenth birthday. First she would pick her up, then they would walk together to school.

Like every day, at the door to Anne's brick apartment building, number 37 Merwedeplein, Hannah had whistled the two notes that signaled her arrival. The door had flown open, sending Anne almost into her arms and both of them into a cascade of giggles.

"You still have two left arms, Hanneli!" Anne had teased.

"*Hartelijk Gefeliciteerd,* Anne! Happy birthday, Anne!" Hannah wished her.

Anne had boasted that now Hannah couldn't tease her about only being twelve, while she was a mighty thirteen, since Hannah was six months older and had reached the grand old age of thirteen first. Anne was happy, her voice ringing.

That day the sitting room of the Frank apartment overflowed with flowers. Anne showed

Hannah a blue blouse that her parents had given to her. She showed gifts from Margot, from Miep at her daddy's office, from Mr. and Mrs. van Daan, from Moortje her cat. They tasted chocolates from a box.

In Anne's bedroom were new games, books, a new red-checkered album, jewelry. Anne admitted that she was spoiled. Looking around, Hannah had seen that it was true. Anne was especially excited to own the red-checkered book that looked like an autograph album.

When Hannah asked if it was an autograph album, Anne explained that she was using it as a diary. Anne had been writing down her secret thoughts with her fountain pen, which had special gray-blue ink. But she never let any of her friends, even Hannah, read what she wrote. Anytime someone asked to see her private writing Anne would hide it with one hand and then tell the busybody, "It's none of your business!" in a flippant way. So, that morning, Hannah hadn't even asked to see what was inside.

After showing her new diary off, Anne had put it with her scrapbooks of cards of the children of kings and queens, and her collection of photos of movie stars. In the sitting room Mr. Frank sat in his favorite soft chair. Hannah liked Mr. Frank. He was lanky, balding, and read the *Joodse Weekblad* just as her own father did.

Mr. Frank had smiled his friendly smile at Hannah. He always made a little joke. Like her own father, Anne's father was no longer allowed to work in his firm in the old part of Amsterdam that produced products for jam and sausage making. Now he spent his days at home. But unlike Mr. Goslar, who was gloomy and pessimistic, Mr. Frank had a cheery disposition.

That day in the newspaper was the order that all Jews must hand in their bicycles by one P.M. on June 24. The bicycle must be in good working condition. Jews must not forget spare tires and tubes. Because thieves had stolen Anne's bicycle, and Mrs. Frank's bicycle and Margot's bike had been hidden, they would not have to hand anything in. It was exhilarating to put one over on the Nazis.

The smell of strong coffee always filled the sitting room. Hannah teased Anne by telling her that even though Anne was finally thirteen, Hannah would always be older. She was already thirteen and a half. When Anne's big eyes were showing their touches of green—a sure sign that Anne was angry—Hannah stopped teasing.

Anne didn't know then, but Hannah, Sanne, Ilse, and Jacque had chipped in together to buy her a book, *Dutch Sagas and Legends,* which they'd present to Anne after school.

The room had been filled with a delicious, fruity odor. Though it was supposed to be a surprise, they knew that Mrs. Frank was baking Anne's favorite strawberry tart for the party.

Before they left, Mrs. Frank had handed Anne a hamper full of sweet biscuits to give to her friends at school. Anne added cookies that she herself had baked. Then Hannah and Anne had walked together to school with the delicious smell of biscuits and cookies rising from the hamper.

In her sleep Mrs. Abrahams shook her. "*Shhh,* Hannah. You're groaning. What's wrong?"

CHAPTER TWENTY-TWO

While visiting her father at the hospital, Hannah saw the obvious, that he was not recovering. She told him about Anne. She told him what Anne had said about gas chambers. She could see he was quite shocked. Though his eyes were glazed, he understood her. Many men visited him because he had helped so many of them when he was still able.

Hannah summoned all her courage and went over to the doctor and looked at him with begging eyes. Her eyes pleaded with him to put them into the next exchange. The doctor was surprised when this gangling brown-haired girl who was all bony arms and legs looked at him like that. It took great courage for a shabby prisoner to make eye contact with a doctor.

When Hannah got back to the barracks, there was great excitement. Packages were being distributed. This had never happened before. The packages were from the Red Cross. Hannah was given two packages for her family. One she immediately hid in order to bring it to her father in the hospital.

The packages were small boxes, the shape and size of a book. When she opened hers, she found dry, fried Swedish bread and dried fruit. Quietly she made a package of things for Anne.

Mrs. Abrahams saw Hannah on her way out of the barracks. She warned her that she mustn't go to the fence again. Once she had been lucky but she might not be so lucky again. Hannah explained that she had made contact with her best friend from her childhood. She told Mrs. Abrahams about Anne Frank, what terrible conditions were on the other side of the fence. Immediately Mrs. Abrahams handed Hannah a few scraps of food to put in the package.

The package consisted of a glove, some Swedish bread and dried fruit, and what she had saved from the evening meal. Hannah waited until it was dark and walked across the camp to the barbed-wire fence. Cautiously she whispered, "Anne? Are you there?"

Immediately the reply came, "Yes, Hanneli, I'm here."

Anne's voice was shaky, and she told Hannah that she had been waiting. Hannah told her she had scrounged up a few things and would throw them over to her.

Hannah felt very weak but summoned her strength and threw the package over the fence.

Immediately there was scuffling noise. Then the sound of someone running and Anne cried out in anguish.

"What happened?"

Anne was crying. "A woman ran over and grabbed it away from me. She won't give it back."

Hannah called, "Anne! I'll try again but I don't know if I'll be able to get away with it."

Anne was crushed.

Hannah begged her to not lose heart, "I'll try. In a few nights. Wait for me."

"I'll wait, Hanneli."

Hannah dashed across the snow, avoiding the searchlight.

CHAPTER TWENTY-THREE

Several days later Hannah was ready to try again. She assembled the remaining Swedish bread, dried fruit, and pieces of food. Again Mrs. Abrahams and a few of the other women in the barracks contributed some precious scraps of food and a pair of socks to the package. It wasn't much, but here it was a fortune.

When she was about to go, someone warned her that there was a moon that would be very bright on the snow. Mrs. Abrahams was fearful for her.

Hannah left the barracks. The moon was bright, the snow was eerie. The searchlight passed. Please, God, Hannah thought, walking to the barbed-wire and straw-filled fence.

She heard her name whispered. "Hanneli? Is that you?"

It was Anne, already waiting.

"Yes, it's me. I'm throwing something over the fence."

She had very little strength, but cast her arm back and threw.

The package sailed over the fence. She heard Anne's excited voice. "I got it!"

Anne gasped to see socks and food. Even a small amount of food could keep a prisoner going for a few more days.

They agreed to meet again soon.

"Until then!" they said at the same moment with one voice, Anne's voice made happy by the package.

Hannah scurried back as fast as she could. There was so much she hadn't yet told Anne, and Anne hadn't told her. Next time, she promised herself. Of course Hannah was very visible in the moonlight, but her luck held.

When she got back to the barracks, not only Mrs. Abrahams but many others were anxiously waiting. They made a place right beside the stove for her. Gabi was awake and squeezed her arms around Hannah urgently. No one had discussed it, but it was commonly known that she could easily be executed for doing what she had just done. Hannah hoped that next time she could find even more food to throw over the wire fence for Anne and Margot.

A few days later the guard pointed to her at roll call and told her that she, her sister, father, and grandmother had been put on the next exchange list. Could it be true? When will the exchange be made? she wanted to know.

"Tomorrow," she was told.

Hannah hurried to the hospital. Her father was so weak. Some of his friends were praying with him. When Hannah told him the news of the exchange, he told one of his friends to go to his barracks and get proper clothes so that he could dress.

It was very obvious that Mr. Goslar was too sick to get dressed, but the man went to fetch his suit anyway. When he returned, Hannah and the nurse helped her father put on his clothes. She looked at him with admiration. He was propped up in his bed in a real suit. He sat with great dignity.

When it was time for Hannah to return to her barracks her father feebly asked her to stay for a minute. "Let's pray together before you go. Let's give thanks for our good fortune."

They prayed together.

The exchange was to take place first thing in the morning. Hannah promised that she and Gabi and Grandma would be ready. She kissed him on his bony forehead and hurried back to her barracks to prepare to leave Bergen-Belsen.

CHAPTER TWENTY-FOUR

Patrols passed by making it impossible to get near the fence to try to say good-bye to Anne. The night, like every night, was noisy with the sound of coughing, groaning, and shallow breathing in the barracks. Before they left at dawn, Mrs. Abrahams promised that she would get a message to Hannah's friend across the fence. "Tell her that surely we'll be back at school this fall . . . only three years behind . . . that I'll see her in Amsterdam!"

It was awful to say good-bye to Mrs. Abrahams and her children.

"Come, Gabi!" Hannah said, and turned away, hurrying through the freezing cold to the hospital.

Inside the hospital, the German doctor saw Hannah and walked over to her. He informed her that during the night her father had died.

Hannah's first thought was, He knew he wasn't strong enough to go. At least he died dressed in proper clothes, knowing that his daughters would be on the exchange transport out of hell. The doctor told her that it was her father's wish that she and her sister and grandmother make the exchange without him.

Hannah took Gabi's hand and hoisted up their rucksack. In a stupor she walked toward the administration building where her grandmother was waiting to report for the exchange.

She and Gabi and Grandmother stood outside in the freezing cold with several hundred people on the exchange list. For four hours they waited, hands and feet numb with the cold. Finally an SS came out of the administration building and announced, "The exchange has been canceled. Go back to your barracks."

Grandmother went back to her barracks and Hannah and Gabi dragged themselves back to theirs. When they arrived, two women covered with sores were after their bed but Mrs. Abrahams put their rucksack back on the bed. Immediately they both collapsed.

It was February 25, 1945.

The stupor continued for some days. During this time Hannah moved around the camp like a sleepwalker. She wasn't asleep but she wasn't awake either. She thought over and over that she was like Anne, without parents. At night she lay on her

back. She must not sink. She was Mama and Papa
to Gabi now.

She prayed. Though her mind was muddy and
she could no longer even think, she knew her father
and mother wouldn't want her to give up. Nor
would God, but she couldn't break out of the tor-
por. She didn't care anymore if she got any food.
All she could think was, I have nobody. I have no
parents anymore. Just like Anne.

She felt dizzy. Her knees buckled and she had
to hold on to a wooden bed frame. Slowly, to get
her balance, she walked back and forth along the
back of the barracks that were filled with the gasps
of the sick prisoners. The dying ones made almost
no noise at all. Rats scurried across the wooden
floor and leaped from bed to bed. Other vermin
had begun to find their way into their barracks, too.

Hannah walked outside. The cold bright un-
feeling moon glared down on the ugly sights of
barbed wire, dirty snow, wooden buildings. There
were so many wooden handcarts filled with dead
bodies now. It was bitter cold. She went toward the
barbed wire to call Anne, to tell her about her father's death.

When she got close someone told her that the
entire section on the other side of the fence had

been emptied. The camp was gone. She stood near the fence and listened. No sounds came from behind the fence. Where had they taken Anne and Margot Frank? There was only the wind, the snow, the stench.

Hannah went back to her barracks. She stood by the stove, afraid that if she lay down, she'd never be able to get back up again. She prayed. When the kettle of soup was brought, Mrs. Abrahams shouted at her, "Eat!"

For Gabi's sake, Hannah made a great effort to do what Mrs. Abrahams said to do.

CHAPTER TWENTY-FIVE

Hannah knew she had typhus. She had a continuous fever, shivers, nausea. She couldn't stand up straight because she was so dizzy. She had seen enough people die of typhus and knew that though her case was still mild, it could easily worsen.

In March, when she was finally able to see Grandmother for a few moment, her grandmother gave her a diamond ring that she'd somehow kept hidden. At the end of March, Grandmother's strength gave out and she died.

In the beginning of April the announcement came that their entire camp was being evacuated. The rumor was that they were being transported to another camp called Theresienstadt. It was whispered that Theresienstadt had gas chambers, that the Nazis wanted to be rid of them all and try to cover up their crimes.

On the day of their departure they were told to pack up their things. Weak as she was, Hannah did so. Mrs. Abrahams did so. Together with the children and several thousand others, they were marched to the train station through gray slush.

Lined up, with a horde of people, they stood and waited for the trains to come. Hannah kept scanning the crowd in case Anne and Margot were being shipped away, too. The moon came up, but still the trains didn't come. Nor was there even a bit of bread to soothe the enormous hunger. Then the moon went down.

It was pitch-black, no stars could be seen. Still, no trains. They stood all night, but no train. Also no Anne or Margot.

Finally, at dawn, the trains arrived. Hannah had never seen such a long train. There must have been fifty cars. The cars were for cattle, not people. In the center was one passenger car filled with German soldiers to guard the trains.

Her group—Mrs. Abrahams, her husband, their seven children, Gabi and she—held on to each other in the hope that they could remain together. They were driven like a herd of animals by the SS into the cattle car. Somehow the Abrahamses were separated from them and put into another car. Hannah recognized a friend of Mrs. Abrahams who also had seven children who had been shoved into the same cattle car with her. This woman was Mrs. Finkel. Most of the other people who were pushed into the cattle car with them were Hungarians.

When the car was full, the sliding door was pulled closed. The only light was a ray through a small opening. It was very crowded; they stood squashed against each other. For a long time they waited. Suddenly the train lurched forward, the wheels ground against the rails. Through the opening they could see barbed wire, willow trees filled with new buds, the big empty field.

The train traveled all day and night. It stopped and started often. The only way they could lie down was to squeeze themselves one next to the other. At night through the opening could be seen fiery incendiaries raining down. Also they heard thunderous explosions made by bombs, but the bombs didn't frighten them any longer. At times the explosions were at a distance, but others were very close.

Suddenly the train jerked to a halt, and the door slid open. A soldier holding a Sten gun shouted, "Get out, run into the fields, get away from the train. Hurry."

The train had stopped in the middle of a farmer's field. Everyone clambered down and ran into the field. Above, airplanes were flying very low and strafing them. The prisoners lay down in the fields and covered their heads. Hannah covered Gabi with her body. People screamed.

Then the airplanes flew on. They were ordered to go back into the trains. Someone who looked like Anne got up from the field, about ten meters away. But when the young woman turned, it wasn't Anne but someone else with dark hair.

As soon as they got back into the cattle car, the doors were shut, and the train began to move again.

CHAPTER TWENTY-SIX

For three days the train stopped and started like that. There was no food, no water, no fresh air, no sanitation. The smell was awful in the dark cattle car. Men and women with lice crawling in and out of hair and eyebrows sank down on the putrid straw and died.

Through the small opening could be seen the passing scenery. On the fourth day they saw red-tinged clouds in the sky. Then the train passed through a very large city where fires were raging. As the train crawled through the city they saw that most of it had been bombed and was in ruins. "It's Berlin!" a man shouted. "Look! The city is destroyed!"

Through the opening they could see Berliners in rags with gray faces. Entire neighborhoods were reduced to piles of rubble. This was the place where Hannah was born in 1928, where her father had been the Deputy Minister of Domestic Affairs and the Chief of Press before the Nazis had won the election, come to power, and begun to persecute Jews.

It was a revelation. So the German people had suffered, too! Hannah thought. Not only us.

Again the train went into the countryside. Then it stopped and the doors were opened. A soldier told them, "If you are strong enough, go into the village and ask the farmers for food."

Mrs. Finkel stayed with Gabi and the children, while Hannah and a few people who could still walk went into the village. They found a farmhouse and begged the farmer for some food. He gave them carrots and some bread. The whole time they were gone, Hannah was very scared that the train would leave without them. When they returned, she decided that she wouldn't ever leave Gabi even though Gabi's belly was swollen from starvation. It was simply too dangerous and she was too feeble. All she could do was go a few steps away to a stream to get some water.

The next time the train stopped, though they were very, very hungry, she refused to go look for food. Mrs. Finkel sent her son while the rest of them waited. As they waited, a trainload of soldiers slowed onto another train track. A German soldier leaned down from a window and held something out to Gabi. Hannah saw that it was a cookie.

Gabi, of course, didn't know what it was.

"Take it," Hannah told her. "Eat it."

Hannah looked up at the soldier. It was the first kind German face she remembered seeing for years. Seeing Gabi's blissful face as her teeth bit into the sweet cookie, Hannah almost went down on her knees before the soldier with thanks before his train passed on.

Shortly they were told to get back onto the train. Mrs. Finkel was agitated, was looking frantically for her son. Just when they were back inside the cattle car, she saw him running across the field. "Wait," Mrs. Finkel screamed at the soldiers who were about to push the door closed, "please!"

But they pushed the door anyway and the train began to move. Mrs. Finkel began pounding the walls and screaming.

Later on, when the train stopped, Hannah realized that if they didn't eat some food soon they would surely die. In the rucksack she'd hidden her grandmother's ring. It had a little diamond. Others began pulling out any valuable possessions that they'd been able somehow to hide because they knew there was very little time left for them. Several had rings, too.

Hannah assembled six valuable rings. She approached a German soldier and told him they needed something to eat. She showed him the six rings.

He took the rings and gave her a little rabbit that was freshly killed. One of the women cooked it on a makeshift fire and they shared it between them. Hannah told Gabi to chew slowly. She wondered where the next food would come from? If they didn't get food, they would shortly die.

For a total of ten days the train went on. They were all at the very end of their endurance. Hannah's supply of strength was completely depleted. She felt so sleepy all the time. Fever burned; she shivered uncontrollably. Her eyes watered.

The urge was to just slip into delirium, but she kept close to Gabi.

Lying next to them, a Hungarian man with fat white lice on his clothes was very sick. He wanted to throw the contents of the slop pot out the hole in the wall. When he reached his arm across her blanket, he lurched and some of the contents spilled on Hannah's blanket.

Hannah got hysterical. She had tried so hard to keep their only blanket clean. It was the one and only time hysteria had overtaken her, and she couldn't control it this time.

When the outburst ended, she gave in to the urge to close her eyes.

CHAPTER TWENTY-SEVEN

When Hannah became aware again, the train was at a standstill. The door was open. Except for a few very sick people and dead people on the filthy floor of the cattle car, everyone else was outside in a field. Gabi, too, was gone.

Hannah pulled herself to her feet and went to the door. Someone shouted at her, "You missed it!"

What had she missed?

"The Germans have surrendered! They were marched away with white flags in their hands!"

She saw that there were no guards anywhere, not one German uniform in sight. Hannah lowered herself to the ground. She found Mrs. Finkel sitting in the field surrounded by her children and Gabi. Mrs. Finkel was too sick and could go no further. She had decided to wait for medical assistance right where the train had stopped, her remaining children with her.

Hannah was too weak to react to the news, her mind was too fuzzy.

Feeble as they were, Hannah and Gabi went to look for food and shelter with a young woman named Mrs. Heilbut. In the group was Mrs. Heilbut's son, and a few others. They stopped near a village named Tröbitz but they couldn't find an empty house. As weak as they were, the group of eight people walked two miles further and came to a village called Schilda. They saw white flags and bedsheets hanging from windows, so they knew the village had surrendered. The Allies had defeated the Germans and their allies! Here Hannah saw the first sight of the victorious Russian Army. They were weary, dirty, soldiers who had been fighting hard to liberate them.

A Russian soldier told them to take the houses of the Nazis. The ragged group walked until they found an empty house. Inside they found potatoes, also jam, but very little else to eat.

Mrs. Heilbut warned them to take care. They mustn't eat too much, or too quickly, since they were in advanced states of starvation. They were to eat only a little or they would die. How awful to die just when they were finally free.

Mrs. Heilbut took Hannah into the garden. She pointed to a tangle of high grasses. "Pick those. We'll use them as a vegetable."

Hannah reached into the tangle and gathered

nettles. Mrs. Heilbut cooked them in a pot. Though Hannah had the urge to eat and drink like a wolf, she drank slowly, ate jam and potatoes and nettles in small amounts. Because Mrs. Heilbut's teeth were rotted away, she could not eat very well.

Mrs. Heilbut noticed that their house belonged to the mayor of the village. Hannah looked into one of the bedrooms. She went into it. In the closet she found a dress for a young girl. The dress was her size. There must have been a girl her age in this house.

She put the dress on. It was a dark wool winter dress. Immediately she crumpled up her filthy old dress. She went outside to the back of the house and threw away the putrid clothes that had long ago turned into rags.

That night Hannah climbed into the girl's bed. It was soft and warm when she hunkered down under the thick feathery eiderdown. The war was really over. As weak as she was, it was like magic to be warm once again. When she looked up she saw a light green tapestry hanging on the wall beside the bed. At the center of the tapestry was printed a dark green swastika. Obviously the house had belonged to Nazis.

Hannah turned her back to the tapestry and fell asleep on her first night of freedom.

CHAPTER TWENTY-EIGHT

A victorious soldier asked, "What is your name?"

She told him, "Hannah Elizabeth Goslar."

"And hers?"

"My sister Gabi."

"How old are you?"

"Sixteen."

"And your sister?"

"My sister was born on October 25, 1940. She's four and a half."

Hannah told him she was Dutch and had been deported from their home in Amsterdam. She didn't want to tell him that she was born in Germany. She felt ashamed of being German. When he asked her if she had any idea of the whereabouts of any other members of her family, she told him that they only had each other. Everyone else was dead, they had no one.

Everywhere were unburied dead covered by blankets. Hannah asked him if he knew the condition of a Mrs. Abrahams who'd been on their transport. He ran his thumb down a list of names and told her that Mrs. Abrahams, her husband, and one son had died shortly after the day of liberation.

Hannah felt terrible. Were Anne or Margot Frank on any of the lists? No. Then he told Hannah and the others to go into the village. He handed out ration cards and told her to use them for food.

At a shop they were given sausage, bread, and milk. One look at their emaciated shapes told the victorious soldiers these people had been in concentration camps. "Eat very little! And eat slowly!" the soldiers warned them because in the very next village were farms and the survivors had found too much food; some had eaten too much and some had died of diarrhea.

A few weeks later a soldier told them to come into the village at eight the next morning with their things.

They did.

Mrs. Heilbut, her son, Hannah, and Gabi were put into military vans with other survivors. The vans drove through the shattered German countryside, past bombed and burned villages, and German people in sorry, miserable states.

The vans arrived at Leipzig. Hannah's group

stayed in a school for several days. Cots and makeshift kitchens had been set up. Others like them arrived, some from Bergen-Belsen and other concentration camps. Hannah kept her eyes open in case Anne or Margot or anyone she knew was in one of the groups.

Three days later they were loaded into a beautiful Red Cross train.

The train moved slowly because of so much damage to the rails. Food was distributed by Red Cross workers. They were serving bacon and eggs and ham and eggs to the passengers. This is my last chance to taste pork, Hannah thought, because she was Kosher, as she was handed a plate full of bacon and eggs. She took a small piece of pink meat on the end of her fork. It wasn't tasty. Next to her was someone eating ham and eggs. She wondered what the ham tasted like?

After several days the train stopped. The sign in the station read MAASTRICHT. She told Gabi that they had reached the Dutch border, but Gabi looked out the window incomprehensibly.

We have no home anymore, Hannah thought, our family is no more.

Outside were houses from which staircases hung in midair because people had used the wood for fuel. Lone figures were riding broken-down black bicycles. The Dutch people looked very worn out indeed. They looked as though they'd been starving, too.

Hannah's group was taken to an old castle. As they were driven along the road to the entrance, a line of healthy Dutch people under a guard of American and Canadian soldiers were being taken away from the castle. Hannah asked who those people were. She was told that they were Dutch Nazis who had collaborated with German Nazis and were being taken away to be punished.

Hannah scrutinized the line of people being marched under guard. They were ordinary-looking men and women. Mrs. Heilbut's son spit out the window at them as they passed.

Everyone lined up and was given clean clothes that had been freshly laundered and smelled like soap. Then they were given shoes. These smelled like real leather. Both were intoxicating odors.

They were taken to be examined by doctors. When Hannah's turn came, the doctor examined her from head to toe. He told her that her lungs were diseased. "You'll have to go directly to the hospital until we can get you into a sanatorium."

"I can't go . . ." Hannah started to say, but Mrs. Heilbut interrupted and told her she'd better go. Gabi could stay with her.

On July 1 Hannah said good-bye to Gabi and was driven to the Maastricht hospital. Waiting for her at the door stood a Catholic nun wearing a flowing white habit. Hannah felt very strange. The nun looked so severe and medieval, but when she gave Hannah a friendly smile Hannah allowed herself to be helped to a little bed with fresh-smelling sheets.

CHAPTER TWENTY-NINE

For many months Hannah stayed in the hospital.

One day a nun came to tell her that she had a visitor. Kind people had donated clothes to everyone in the hospital, so Hannah had some nice clothes to wear. She was wearing a freshly laundered dress that showed how much her figure had matured during the past two years, how long and shapely her legs were. Her hair had grown lustrous again.

Behind the nun was Anne Frank's father, Otto Frank.

Hannah couldn't believe her eyes. "I think that your daughters are alive!" she told him.

His face got ashen.

Hannah told him she'd spoken with Anne at Bergen-Belsen right before the end, that Anne was alive though Margot had been very sick.

Quietly he told her that he, too, had been hopeful but a short time ago he had received a letter from a woman who wrote that she had been with Anne and Margot at the end in Bergen-Belsen. He told her that Anne and Margot had not survived.

They sat down close together.

It was so unfair, Hannah thought. Anne had made it right to the end. It couldn't have been more than a few weeks before the war ended that she had seen Anne. She must have died right before the liberation. Hannah looked at Anne's father. She felt sure that if Anne had known that her father was alive she would have found the strength to go on.

Mr. Frank explained that he'd seen Hannah's name on a list of survivors. He'd also seen Jacque in Amsterdam, she was all right. He had no news of Ilse or Sanne, just that they had been deported, too. He told her that transportation conditions were so bad that it had taken him eight hours to get from Amsterdam to Maastricht instead of the usual one and a half hours.

In September Hannah was brought from the hospital in Maastricht straight to the Joodse Invalide Hospital in Amsterdam. The high building once had belonged to the Jews of Amsterdam. It had been taken by the Nazis but was given back after the war. Hannah was still very ill.

Some floors were hospital floors, others were for orphans.

She met the Heilbuts again. Gabi was in an orphanage nearby, and was getting strong. A grown-up Jacque came to visit; so did Hannah's friend Iet Swillens, who brought Hannah a few photos including one of Anne Frank's birthday party.

Mrs. Goudsmit came to visit. She brought Hannah an album of the Goslar family photographs which must have been left with her for safekeeping. Hannah thanked her for this priceless gift and also for the book on Florence Nightingale that she'd sent to her in Westerbork.

She was too ill to go to her old neighborhood but didn't really want to anyway. She'd heard that after they were deported, the Germans took all their possessions and sent them to Germany, and new people had moved into their apartment. Even though the war had ended, these people remained in the apartment.

She found out that Alfred Bloch had been sent to Mauthausen concentration camp and had never been heard from again by anyone. Sanne and Ilse, like Anne, Margot, and Mrs. Frank, had also not come back from the camps. With each passing day the lists of murdered victims—Jewish and also Christian—grew longer.

Mr. Frank came often and visited. Hannah remembered how she and Anne used to watch him pour beer into his glass when Hannah came over for dinner. She reminded him how they'd held their breath in the hope that the foam would run over the top of his glass but it never had. Speaking of these moments made points of pink stand out on his cheeks.

He told Hannah that he had arranged for her to go to a sanatorium in Switzerland because she was still very sick and needed a long time to recuperate. Because the only surviving member of Hannah's family, her uncle, was also in Switzerland, it was possible to get documents for her and Gabi to go.

CHAPTER THIRTY

On November 12, 1945, Hanneli turned seventeen. On December 5, Mr. Frank came to fetch her by taxi. On the way to the airport he picked up Gabi at the orphanage and two other children who had an aunt in Switzerland. Hannah had never been on an airplane before but was not scared at all. Instead she was curious about what it would feel like to fly up into the sky.

The small airplane stood on the tarmac. While the little group waited, Mr. Frank handed Hannah and the others Dutch coins on a chain. He slipped them over their heads. On one side was the face of the queen. On the other side was engraved the date of their journey—December 5, 1945.

Hannah and Mr. Frank spoke quietly together.

Hanneli remembered that when she and Anne were small, she was as guilty as Anne of chattering at school but because Anne was so peppery, and Hanneli so sugary, it was always Anne who caught the sharp edge of the teachers' anger. Never

Hanneli, whose reputation was that she was shy, sweet, and obedient. But Anne had always said that Hanneli was shy on the outside but spunky with people close to her. Anne knew Hannah better than anyone, and had loved to tease her.

Mr. Frank told Hannah that when they were in hiding Anne had often talked about Hannah. He told her that Anne regretted so much that she hadn't said good-bye to Hannah, that they hadn't sorted out all their differences before Anne went into hiding. Hannah was Anne's oldest friend and he hoped he and Hannah would be good friends and always stay in touch. He would like to be like a second father to her.

Hannah wished she knew what Anne's thoughts about her had been while Anne was in hiding and had had so much time to think and reflect. But how could she ever know Anne's thoughts? How could she ever know if Anne felt the rift between them had healed? How could she ever again come close to a friend in that same way? Already Hannah was seventeen, almost grown up, and Anne—forever—would remain a girl.

Mr. Frank walked Hannah and the children to the airplane. He wished them a good journey. He waited on the tarmac while they walked up the little stairway into the plane. Hannah quickly settled the little girls in seats, and put Gabi next to her. Shortly the engines began to growl, and the propeller to turn. The airplane rolled forward. Through the window Mr. Frank could be seen as he stood alone and waved. Then the plane taxied, and Hannah realized that it was flying up into the air.

Hannah's stomach jumped with excitement. She gripped Gabi by the hand. The earth seemed to fall away. Outside were red roofs, and green and brown fields striped by ribbons of water. Canals. Elm trees in a line. The Dutch countryside. There were the spires of small village churches, thatched cottages, redbrick houses. The airplane made a wide turn, and off in the distance was the irregular coastline, the dark green North Sea. Boats. An orange smudge of sunset.

In Hannah's suitcase was the photo album that Maya Goudsmit had saved from her family's apartment after the arrest. It was the only surviving remnant of her past, preserved for her by an act of kindness. In the book were photos of her parents. They were smiling, young, newly married. There were photographs of her grandparents, her uncle.

There were photos of her infant years in Berlin before Adolf Hitler was elected in 1933.

There were photos of Amsterdam, a photo of

Hannah and Anne on the sidewalk in front of the apartment on Merwedeplein. Age ten. This was the time when Mr. Frank often took Hannah and Anne with him to his office on Sundays.

Anne and Hanneli had played in the big room. They'd called each other on the telephone, played with a stamp that had the date, rolled paper into the typewriter, and wrote letters to each other. They dropped water on people who were on the street. What fun it was to be naughty with Anne!

While they played, the clear bell of the Westerkerk church down the street rang every fifteen minutes.

Though she had not known it at the time, this very office would be Anne's hiding place for over two years.

There was a photo of five little girls from school sitting in a sandbox. Hannah had a big bow in her hair, Anne had knobby knees. The year, 1937.

Another showed nine girls with their arms around each other, 1939.

There was a photo of Hannah and Mr. Goslar, 1935.

There was a photo of Mrs. Goslar.

There was a photo of the thatched cottage in which the Goslars rented rooms during the summer on the North Sea when Anne came to stay. There were photos of Gabi and Hannah. Gabi was born just as the German army had attacked and occupied Holland, 1940. The photographs demonstrated that the Nazis hadn't stopped them altogether from enjoying life.

Hannah and Anne had pushed Gabi's carriage, proud to be allowed to take Gabi for strolls up and down the neighborhood streets that bordered on the Amstel River. They had pretended that Gabi belonged to them, had taken turns pushing the carriage, and sometimes both pushed at once. They'd always have the same conversation on these walks.

Hannah clearly remembered every word of this conversation:

"How many children do you want?" Anne would ask her.

"I want ten children," Hannah would reply. "What about you?"

"I don't know how many, but I'm planning to be a writer."

"I know. And Margot wants to be a nurse in Palestine."

"Right. And you want to sell chocolates in a shop, or teach history. Right?"

"Right."

Another time, walking along the elm-lined

park path, Gabi had fallen asleep and they'd decided to sit for a while. They'd walked on toward the bench but when they'd come to it, the bench had a new sign: FORBIDDEN FOR JEWS.

At that moment it seemed like the Nazis had declared war on them. But why? What had they ever done? Baffled, angry to be persecuted so unfairly, they had left the park, and never went back after that.

While so many people had not survived, the photographs were safe in her suitcase. Though memory might blur, the photos would remain unchanged.

The earth fell away further as the airplane veered and climbed into rain-filled Dutch clouds. A confetti of silvery raindrops streaked the little windows. The plane began to bump and shake and flew through thick, dark clouds. It took a while to fly through the rainstorm.

By then night had come and the plane flew into the dark. Outside were strewn clusters of shining stars. There was the Little Dipper constellation, like an upside-down kite. It had seven pulsating stars. To Hannah the stars had names: Sanne, Ilse, Jacque, and Hannah. At the tip of its tail was the bright Pole Star that the first sailors once used to navigate at night. This star was Anne.

As Hanneli's plane flew on toward Switzerland, the constellations gradually climbed. The plane climbed, too. New stars rose over the earth's horizon and the pulsating old stars moved majestically, eternally across the heavens.